The SEDUCTION of EXTREMES

The SEDUCTION of EXTREMES

SWALLOWING CAMELS AND STRAINING GNATS

PETER KUROWSKI

Pleasant Word (a division of WinePress Publishing, PO Box 428, Enumclaw, WA 98022) functions only as book publisher. As such, the ultimate design, content, editorial accuracy, and views expressed or implied in this work are those of the author.

ISBN 13: 978-1-4141-0644-1
ISBN 10: 1-4141-0644-0
Library of Congress Catalog Card Number: 2005910346

Dedication

To my brother pastors of the Jefferson City and Columbia Circuits of the Missouri District of The Lutheran Church – Missouri Synod, and Dr. Wilbert Rosin, friend and mentor.

> "Behold, how good and pleasant it is when brothers dwell in unity!"
> —Psalm 133:1

Table of Contents

Acknowledgments

Thanks to Twilla Duvall, Elena Jungmeyer, Morgan Clennin, Daniel Hartman, Samuel Powell, and my wife, Janice, for editorial assistance.

Thanks to Lewis Pritchett, James L. Ramer, and Dr. John Oberdeck for reviewing the book.

Thanks to Dr. Paul L. Maier and Dr. John Warick Montgomery for their kind words of endorsement.

Thanks to Pastor Gerald Scheperle, Pastor Steve Riordan, and Pastor Nabil Nour for words of encouragement.

Thanks to the staff at WinePress Publishing for making this a better book.

Thanks to Paul Kuester for supporting this project.

Foreword

In matters theological, what ever happened to moderation in all things—shunning the extremes, staying on the royal road in avoiding the ditches of fanaticism to the right and to the left by pursuing the Golden Mean? In the sixteenth century, Luther used to complain about the *rabies theologorum*, the madness of theologians who doggedly rode their doctrinal hobbyhorses off the Middle Way and into ditches on the right and left.

A survey of today's cultural landscape shows that little has changed. Extremism is alive and well in the 21st century, particularly in the areas of politics and religion. Christianity is Peter Kurowski's prime concern in these pages, and he finds it a veritable battleground between the far right and the far left, all rooted in what he felicitously terms TDD for Tension Deficit Disorder. He is enjoying some word play, of course, on ADD or Attention Deficit Disorder. Because our faith is loaded with a precious procession of paradoxes, failure to keep these paradoxes in balance—in tension with each other—leads to easy espousal of one extreme or the other.

With care, the author seeks to show that one can take the path of the golden middle without being a fence sitter. Enlisting the cross of Christ as the balancing beam of the universe, one can find equilibrium for walking the high wire of life. Proper understanding of the good news of Jesus' love helps one to avoid strict legalism and open libertinism, cheapened grace and cheap grace, totalitarianism and anarchy, hopeless pessimism and hapless utopianism. Dozens more of these polarity pitfalls this parish pastor identifies on these illuminating pages.

Rich in illustration, rippling with clever word play, and squarely on-target in so many instances, The Seduction of Extremes is a fresh, impressive way to understand our faith and avoid perilous doctrinaire pitfalls in going off the deep end to either the right or the left. Understanding the paradoxes of Christianity also helps enormously in dealing with some of the problems and logical difficulty skeptics always seem to raise in attacking our faith.

Moreover, it is not just skeptics raising obstacles. Recently, a professor at a Lutheran seminary, someone who should have known better, urged a virtual doctrine of double predestination on his classes with the following logic: "If God predestines some to salvation, He, in effect, condemns the others." While this statement has good logic, it is bad theology! Clearly, this supposedly Lutheran professor was a Calvinist in fact for failing to note the divine paradox involved here, although Luther saw it very clearly. Similarly, logic tells us that one does not equal three in the Trinity—another paradox—or that the infinite God could become finite in Jesus, the ultimate paradox. While simple logic cries, faith affirms both since faith understands and celebrates the necessary tensions of Christianity that keep the extremes in balance.

You may not agree with everything in these pages—I questioned the text in several places—but generally, this is a breath of fresh air that should improve the sometimes-fetid atmosphere of current theological debate. It surely will help us avoid those oh-so-unnecessary extremes that clutter the Christian world today.

Paul L. Maier
Seibert Professor of Ancient History
Western Michigan University

Chapter 1

Tension Deficit Disorder

A long time ago, an apt observer of history and humanity made this judgment. He said that man, by nature, is like a drunken peasant riding on a horse. He rides a few yards and falls into a ditch on the right. After a rude lesson on gravity, he gets back up and rides a little farther only to fall next in the ditch on the left. Right. Left. Right. Left. All the way along, the zigzagging drunk continues this right/left fall-guy routine. We never do find out if the poor chap made it back home.

Throughout the world, we see radical groups, rabid religious movements, and intense ideologues suffering severely from the drunken peasant syndrome. Take two well-known extremes—the North American Man-Boy Love Association (NAMBLA) and Muslim terrorists. Members of both would have been immensely sympathetic toward taking similar steps that led to the French Revolution. Predatory policies mark their manner. Adult sex with under-aged children is not necessarily forbidden fruit. Each sector makes extreme pleasure the measure to obtain their treasure. Thus, they are hedonists in drag. One group is willing to fly suicidal missions with the hellish hope of falling into the arms of 72 virgins. The other group believes that sodomy with anyone or anything could be the road to nirvana.

NAMBLA believes in utopian pleasure and freedom without responsibility even though history teaches that this is a formula for anarchy that then morphs into totalitarianism. On the teeter-totter of life, you must have a balance between rights and responsibilities. Out of touch with reality, NAMBLA goes so far as to advocate the legalization of sex between men and boys as young as eight years old.[1]

On the other side of extremism are the 120 million Muslim fanatics around the world who want to advance their Caliphate by sword, suicide, and savagery. While the majority of Muslims are peace-loving people, this large minority of fascists is not content with an equal seat at the table of life; they want the whole table.

Whether NAMBLA (a group of vile radicals supported by people on the far, far left) or Muslim fascists (bile-radicals on the far, far right), a common pattern emerges. Neither group is open to reason. Neither group is open to a wholesome rule of law. Whether the tyranny of a majority, as in the case of militant Muslims, or the terrorism of a minority, as in the case of NAMBLA, you find a kinship of evil and a fellowship of lawlessness. Neither group understands what love truly means. Neither group can rise to the level of what the architects of our nation said was the bare minimum for good government—organized selfishness. In the end, the health of the commonwealth is not on the radar screen of a fanatic.

Extremism is a growing characteristic of our culture. Increasingly, the common good is little understood. In American politics, extremism manifests itself by way of incivility. Recently, former three-term U.S. Senator Jack Danforth took to task political liberals and conservatives for their increasingly snide, coarsening conversation. Danforth realizes that reckless language that goes for tissue rather than issue does not adorn freedom but rather deifies demagoguery. It is more Hitler-like than Lincoln-like. Extreme rhetoric, in the end always aids and abets in the collapse of basic standards of decency.

Christendom has not escaped these toxic fumes of extremism. As a result, huge confusion reigns throughout all major church bodies.

Rather than being God's pleasantly peculiar people grounded in the gospel, Christians are often pendulum people staggering into ditches. Some church bodies have ditched so much of their theological core they have rolled down into the valley of irrelevance. Along the way, perceived needs have trundled over real needs. Tactics have trampled truth as an ultimate concern.

A key reason for the descent into chaos and extremism is widespread Biblical illiteracy. George Barna is a nationally renowned researcher who specializes in studying American views on religion and religious matters. According to Barna, about 1 in 30 Americans holds to a Biblical worldview.[2] Roman Catholic scholar Michael Novak, in his book *"On Two Wings,"* documents carefully how formative the Bible was upon the thinking of early Americans. Reason and revelation were the two wings of the American eagle. According to Novak, "Before Sidney and Locke, Americans had fashioned a political doctrine from the Hebrew Bible…It is less true to say that America was Lockean…than that Locke was American."[i]

This radically deadly departure from the foundation of our nation's beginnings needs more biopsy. Any serious study of primary source documentation of the worldview of the framers and founders of our nation will reveal how the vast majority of our leaders shared a Biblical worldview, parochial views and philosophical currents not withstanding. Most of the key contributors read regularly the Greek New Testament. James Madison could not only handle well Greek and Latin, but the last courses he imbibed while at Princeton were in the Hebrew Scriptures. John Eidsmoe in his careful work, *"Christianity and the Constitution: The Faith of our Founding Fathers,"* documents how the framers and founders took pains to avoid a form of government that would end up on some extreme point of the political continuum. Drawing foremost from the Bible in general and the book of Deuteronomy (the second giving of the law) in particular, they quietly enlisted the wisdom of these writings to avoid two extremes. One, they wanted to avoid a theocracy—a specific religion-run government—such as the form of government that militant

Islam seeks to establish. Two, they wanted to avoid complete separation of church and state so as not to make the French mistake resulting in that country's reign of terror.

In order not to be seduced by extremes, the framers of our constitution would set forth a form of government that sought to live with a vital tension. They would form a government that, on the one hand, would evince a certain kind of institutional separation and yet, on the other hand and at the same time, allow for functional interaction. The genius of this disposition flows from the beautiful nature of the Hebrew and Greek Scriptures of the Bible. In essence, the Bible teaches human beings all about balance, all about living with tension, and all about avoiding extremes. If the sacred Scriptures are not ripped out of context, not treated like a smorgasbord, and not misquoted, one will witness in them a spirit that moves people to seek the authentic golden middle.

Granted, even in the very best state of affairs, history is untidy, passions easily given to extremes, and the very best of human beings have major moments when they lose their equilibrium. Nevertheless, the founders and framers of our nation had a moment of enlightenment, clarity, and courage. To pull off this noble experiment of a democratic republic they banked upon influencing a critical mass of people with a Hebrew-Christian worldview. Without this, there could not be the necessary citizenry to form "a more perfect union." Had the thinking of the French Revolution rather than Biblical revelation been in American air, the thirteen colonies would have inherited a daughter called anarchy and a granddaughter called totalitarianism. Robespierre would have fathered the one and Napoleon the other.

Today, little by little, our Biblically illiterate masses are gravitating toward worldviews that spell either the extreme of anarchy or the excess of totalitarianism. Because of this drift from a common interpreter to reality, the Bible's moral common ground is eroding, the common good shrinking, and a sense of the commonwealth disappearing. At the same time, most Americans are buying into *isms* that either lack moral boundaries or have precious little to say about God's boundless love in Jesus Christ.

Even where you have people seriously studying the Bible, there is yet another problem. Often, you hear a sermon, read a devotional writing, or study a major theological paper and you see another tragic pattern. One truth from the Bible is pressed excessively far at the expense of a balancing truth. It has been said that heresy is nothing more than a truth exaggerated. Invariably when heresy arises, the person and work of Jesus gets short shrift. When this happens, the balance of the message that Jesus brings, as well as the brilliance he offers, departs from a culture. Without the light of Christ, the pure gives way to the pornographic, the noble gives way to the narcissistic, and truth gets twisted like a waxen nose.

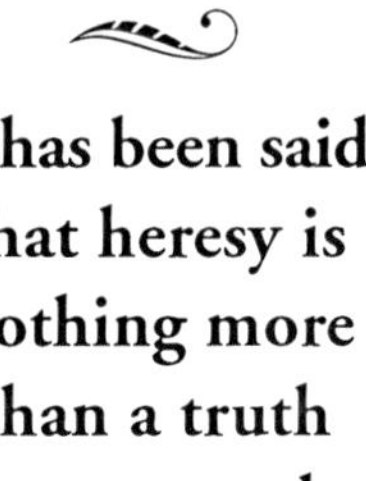

It has been said that heresy is nothing more than a truth exaggerated.

Truth, like the disciples of Jesus, goes out two by two. In a yin and yang fashion, the cardinal teachings of the Bible seek to help humans avoid drifting too far to the right and too far to the left. From Genesis to Revelation, the Holy Spirit carves a consistent coherent paradoxical path. That path continually weaves between the excesses of salvation-by-works manifestos and do-your-own-thing declarations of independence. In so doing, the Bible sets itself apart from all other holy books in history.

"That which is orthodox is paradox" is an ancient axiom. A paradox is the wedding of two seemingly contradictory truths that form a deeper truth. The bride of Christ, the church, is a resurrection result of a wedding born through an engagement of gospel paradoxes. This should not surprise anyone who is a disciple of the absolute paradox, Jesus Christ. From his person to his passion to his parables, the life, work, and teachings of Jesus exude paradox.

St. Paul reminds us that the heart of the good news of Jesus is high paradox. Writing to the Romans, Paul reveals how God declares the ungodly godly. (Romans 4:5) God does this for the sake of his Son who, though rich, became poor that through his poverty all people could become rich. (2 Corinthians 8:9) He does this because of a paradox Martin Luther called "the happy exchange." On the cross, Jesus takes on his sinless shoulders (1 Peter 2:22) all of our sin. In return, he freely grants forgiveness, life, and salvation. (2 Corinthians 5:18-19, Luke 23:34, 43) This is the great evangelical exchange!

This good news changes the attitudes of those who take it to heart. To know that we are not the random jazz dance of the molecules, but rather objects of God's intense love is the juice behind the central Biblical doctrine of justification. Brennan Manning's *"The Ragamuffin Gospel"* expands the meaning behind this prime time paradox:

> "Justification by grace through faith" is the theologian's learned phrase for what Chesterton called "the furious love of God." He is not moody or capricious; He knows no seasons of change. He has a single relentless stance toward us: He loves us. He is the only God man has ever heard of who loves sinners. False gods—the gods of human manufacturing—despise sinners, but the Father of Jesus loves all, no matter what they do. However, this is almost too incredible for us to accept. Nevertheless, the central affirmation of the Reformation stands: Through no merit of ours, but by His mercy, the life, death and resurrection of God's beloved Son restores us to a right relationship with God. This is the Good News, the gospel of grace.[4]

The nature of this good paradoxical news is that, at the same time, it helps us fight two spiritual seductresses. Each seductress leads to self-worship. Each is an opposite in one way but a clone in another. Both are hollow, hellish hookers the devil uses to pull people away from God's most dramatic display of love in history—the cross. The first seductress is Lady Legalism. Her lethal sister is Lady Lawlessness. In the spiritual realm, legalism is the narcissistic notion that human beings earn our way to heaven in some measure by fulfilling the law of God. The teaching of justification rules out this self-flattering noxious notion. After all, God justifies, declares not guilty the ungodly. This is sheer grace. (Ephesians 2:8-9) It is pure gift. (James 1:17) The sad reality is that the only thing human beings contribute to salvation is their sin.

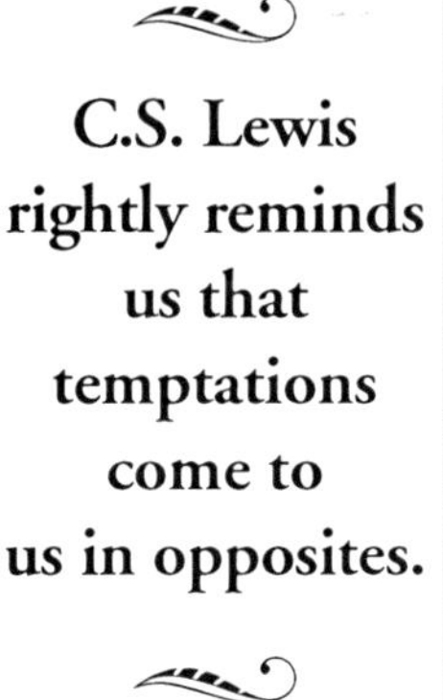

On the other hand, we face the opposite danger of seduction by Lady Lawlessness. C.S. Lewis rightly reminds us that temptations come to us in opposites. If we are not fending off Lady Legalism, we are fleeing Lady Lawlessness. Actually, legalism is just one more form of lawlessness. St. Paul writes, "By the works of the law shall no flesh be justified." (Galatians 2:16) Here the law of God teaches it is lawless to teach salvation by the law when it comes to mere human beings.

The whole purpose of Jesus, as true God and true man when he came into the world, was not only to take away our sin (1 John 1:7) but also to perfectly fulfill the law. (Matthew 5:17) Paul argues that if righteousness could come any other way than Jesus, then Jesus died needlessly. (Galatians 2:21) The good news of Jesus is that there is even more good news yet to come. Salvation is full and free. Jesus fulfilled the law for us, but when this salvation connects with his love, it produces new creations, not dead stumps. The Bible says, "If anyone is in Christ, he is a new creation." (2 Corinthians 5:17) Christ's great Good Friday love moves followers to walk in love as well as celebrate justification by grace through faith.

Despite so much confusion in the Christian church today, I thank God for the implications of this paradoxical truth of justification. It assures followers of Jesus that our perfect Savior, not our perfect faith, saves us. St. Paul affirms this truth when he writes, "For no one can lay a foundation other than that which is laid, which is Jesus Christ." (1 Corinthians 3:11)[5] Nevertheless, the core paradoxical teaching of justification should signal how a gospel-centered disposition will eschew all extremes. It frees people from the curse of the law, (Galatians 3:10) from eternal death, (Romans 6:23) from the tyranny of the Devil, (Ephesians 6:12, 13, Colossians 1:13) and frees us to live lives in step with freedom. (Galatians 5:1)

There is more good news. The beauty of paradox in service of the gospel is it alerts Christians to another reality. It reveals that the characteristics of orthodoxy are faithfulness as well as flexibility. To some, this might seem like a contradiction. Yet, properly understood, the substance of the gospel is like the strand on which a high wire walker travels. If one end or the other of the wire, one theological strand or its opposite, does not have equal tension, the wirewalker will have a most difficult journey. Lapse of tension will lead to collapse of the person. Consequently, the wirewalker may easily lose balance and tumble either to the right or to the left.

St. Paul offers sound counsel to fend off the seduction toward extremes. Paul's paradoxical mind will not yield an inch when it comes to sacrificing any of the fabulous facets of this paradoxical good news. (Galatians 1:6-9) At the same time, this same apostle is willing to bend over backwards wherever possible to advance this Good News. (1 Corinthians 9:22-27) He will bend over backwards short of compromising aspects of this balancing, comforting Good News. Rightly understood, Paul's motto, after coming to know of Jesus' love and pardon, could have been, "In essentials unity, in nonessentials liberty, and in everything charity."

The key here is to know the essentials. Know the core and know the score. St. Paul, in his epistle to the Romans, identifies the gospel in all its articles as the power of God unto salvation. (Romans 1:16) Equally important, love—the prime of the fruit of the gospel—is to accompany what and how one believes, teaches, and confesses. (1 Corinthians 13)

In my own Lutheran Church—Missouri Synod we have struggled in recent decades to maintain theological balance. At times, we have bought into a gospel reductionism (a reduced gospel). At other times, we have bought into a gospel restrictionism (a reduced playing field in spreading the gospel).[6] In an ideal fallen world, brothers and sisters on each side would sit down and lovingly get on the same theological page. Instead, each side frequently gets hijacked by saints who argue for excesses.[7] Dr. Paul Maier, our denomination's second vice president, answers the question: How did we get into this situation?

> Extremism, pure and simple. Extremism is a curse in the public sector, the private sector, and especially also in the church. Two extremist poles, with many gradations in between, seem to influence the way people think and act. The pole on the extreme left is a radical open-mindedness that opposes strictures of all kinds, scoffs at tradition, is antinomian if not libertine, and worships change for the sake of change. The pole on the extreme right is a radical close-mindedness that detests change, lives by the Law and is severely judgmental and suspicious of all not so minded.[8]

This book will try to identify this core. To maintain theological balance implies knowing the center of Biblical theology. Apart from locating the center, it is hard avoiding the drunken peasant syndrome. Where can one adapt, change, improvise, and improve the application of one's theology? Where must one draw the line lest one falls headlong into the ditch of legalism or lawlessness? As one whose doctoral thesis was in the field of paradox, I know this is not an easy task. Ultimately, only the Holy Spirit can help us find the theological sweet spot.

Elton Trueblood, a Christian apologist and philosopher, wrote of the value of paradox in the formulation of religious truth. About the brilliant French thinker Blaise Pascal's apt use of paradox, Trueblood said:

> Almost as important as the idea of involvement is the idea of paradox, this has been a common theme in religious thought, but was particularly prominent in the brilliant notes left by Pascal when he died. The heart of the idea is this: Because truth is never simple, it is usually necessary, when dealing with profound matters, to present at least two propositions rather than one. Often the two propositions are in

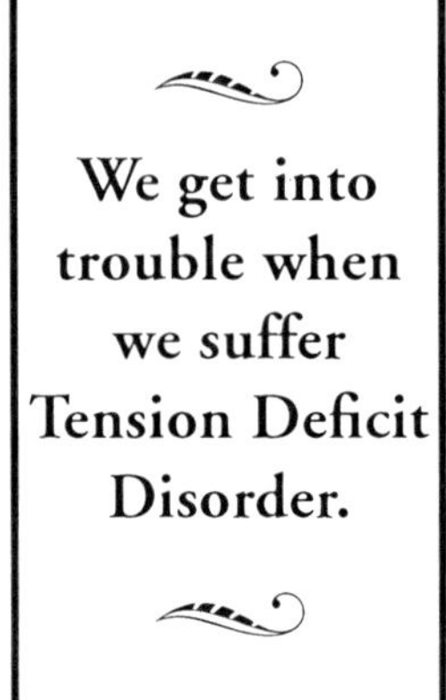

We get into trouble when we suffer Tension Deficit Disorder.

sharp tension, but this is essential to the effort to represent adequately the complexity of the situation.[9]

The paradoxical good news of Jesus produced within Paul a spirit that was yielding and unyielding at the same time. Bear in mind that at one time Paul had been completely unyielding. At one time Paul was an extremist, a fanatic, and a man who murdered people for not believing his version of Judaism. Then this theological terrorist met the risen Christ. (Acts 9)[10] Christ's love profoundly changed Paul. Christ's love enlightened Paul to see major paradoxes that Paul at one time did not have on his radar screen.

Faith in the absolute paradox, Jesus, caused the scales of extremism to fall off Paul's eyes. The Holy Spirit gave to Paul a new spirit. This new spirit recognized that in Christ the apostle's weakness became strength, the child of God lives by dying, and that God reveals to conceal so the life of the child of God might truly be one of faith. Paul would learn that this same Savior gives us a choice in matters of faith but God never excludes our decisions from His all-encompassing grace. In short, the nature of the gospel is that it helps us to hold ferocious opposites in tension to deal with the tensions of life.

We get into trouble when we suffer Tension Deficit Disorder.[11] Tension Deficit Disorder occurs when we let go of one truth and hold on to the opposite truth as it goes spinning out of control from centrifugal force. We drift, as Moses would put it, too far to the right or too far to the left. (Deuteronomy 5:32) When that happens we end up in an orbit that moves away from the Son, who is the center of the universe. (Colossians 1:15-20)

Tension Deficit Disorder (TDD) is a major malady of our age. Its powers of seduction are intoxicating. Years ago Tony Campolo identified the seductive power of extremes when he wrote the thoughtful book,

"Partly Right." The full title of the book reads, *"We Have Met the Enemy and They are Partly Right."* In his book, Campolo shows how enemies of the church such as Nietzsche, Marx, Freud, and Hegel often had some legitimate critiques of how Christendom plays out. They were partly right. Unfortunately, they usually based their critiques on a version of Christianity that is not in step with the Bible and the good news of Jesus. They became experts in analyzing caricatures. They excelled at using half-truths to torch half-truths.

In addition, the partly right critics veered into philosophical wastelands for another reason. Tragically, they gave in too easily to either/or categories rather than timely both/and formulas. Rather than holding in tension two or more good truths that were balancing yet opposite, they fall prey to Tension Deficit Disorder. They ended up in halfway houses built by the great seducer of half-truths—Satan, the Father of Lies. An ally to the ego of one-track philosophers, the devil excels in mixing truth with error. Throughout the ages, he has delighted in seductive entrapment using partial truths as his bait. His modus operandi is to dress up deadly error in the garments of piecemeal truth.

In Jesus' day, our Lord repeatedly faced a brigade of half-truth experts. The extremists in his day often were dogmatic in peripherals, but had lost the core meaning of the Hebrew Scriptures. They overlooked the fact that salvation resided in Yahweh's gift of righteousness. (Psalm 31:1; 72:2)

Intoxicated by the illusion of salvation by works, the extremists mastered in nitpicking to death the poor, but flunked the basics when it came to love, compassion, and fairness. Jesus took dead aim at the hairsplitting, atomistic attempts of one-upmanship and control. One of his seven woes, before he quickened his steps on a paradoxical path to the cross, said it all. Seeking to call religious leaders back to their senses, Jesus said, "Woe to you, scribes and Pharisees.... You blind guides, straining out gnats and swallowing a camel." (Matthew 23:23a, 24)

Unfortunately, throughout Christendom there is no shortage of straining out gnats and swallowing camels. Prophets of triviality abound. Through ADD—Attention Deficit Disorder of a theological kind—they do not pay close attention to what the Holy Spirit says in Scripture. Good exegetes—men and women who read out of the Greek and Hebrew the meaning of God's Word—will make every effort not to add to or subtract from the sacred text. Good exegetes also know that context is king when seeking to draw the meaning of Scripture. If you are inattentive to the text and its context, a person can easily bear false witness to God's Word.

Now add TDD to ADD. This is double trouble. If people do not grasp the paradoxical patterns of the whole of Scripture, or pay close attention to the text of Scripture, reckless interpretations of the Bible arise. Good exegetes help us avoid ADD. Good systematic scholars help us avoid TDD. Faithful systematic scholars will try to point out the paradoxical pathways that run throughout the Bible. This helps a person to see what looks at first glance like a seeming contradiction is really a paradox.

In our day and age of slogans and sound bytes, people rarely get a full spiritual diet that helps one to contend vigorously with the seduction of the extremes. This book will make an effort to assist people interested in understanding central teachings of the most balanced book in the world, the Bible. It will seek to demonstrate how, as Augustine noted, the Bible is like an ocean, simple enough for a child to wade into and deep enough to drown an elephant. Above all, the sound of Scripture is a paradoxical symphony telling the story of how a paradoxical king has come to earth to give human beings meaning, joy, and eternal life. Apart from this story, the fairy tales take over and the seduction of extremes continues to leave us under endless tyrannies.

Chapter 2

PRESUPPOSITIONS

Before I get up a head of steam, I need to state a few things about my background and approach. First, I am a Lutheran Christian. I hope you will not hold that against me. Keep in mind that most Lutherans are not Lutherans. Let me put it another way. Most people who take the name *Lutheran* have little idea what historic Lutheranism is about. Many have never received instruction on the ABC's of Lutheranism. Others have long abandoned their evangelical roots. Here's the nub. You cannot judge most Lutherans by their logo. Ergo, what you may know about Lutheranism may not be Lutheran whatsoever. Yet, what is true of Lutheranism in terms of members drifting from roots is true of most Presbyterians, Roman Catholics, Episcopalians and Christians in general.[12] Most Christians know very little of the denomination from which they come. That is one of the factors making everything so difficult to assess today.

Two, I have learned a tremendous amount from Christians of other denominations. I am a Lutheran Church—Missouri Synod pastor who has prayer partners who are Catholic priests, Baptist pastors, Episcopalian priests, Methodist ministers, as well as liberal and conservative Lutheran clergy alike. True Lutherans, I believe, cherish this kind of ecumenism with fellow members of the household of faith. Yes, there are areas where, for the sake of the gospel and the sake of conscience, one must draw lines regarding participation when it comes to certain events. That topic we hope to wrestle with later! However, orthodox Lutherans do not believe we will be the only gang in heaven. That very idea will gag a good Lutheran. At times, donkey prophets pin that heresy on our tails, but the idea is abhorrent to all thoughtful Lutherans. Remember, we confess that our perfect Savior saves us, not our perfect faith. Regardless of Christian denomination, all people who believe that Jesus Christ is Lord—the risen Savior of the world—will receive salvation. (Acts 16:31) In fact, there are even people in cults and non-Christian religions who will be saved in spite of their religions, not because of them. By virtue of what theologians refer to as the happy inconsistency, they come to faith in Jesus as Savior and Lord despite the high heresy that is the official position of their religion.

At the same time, I refuse to pray with some so-called Christian clergy. Let me explain. Years ago, we had one clergyman in our little town in which I served a country congregation. At any rate, this minister was telling the children of his church that Lutherans were cannibals. Of course, these children began to act toward the children in our Lutheran congregation as if they were cannibals because, as he explained to them, Lutherans believe that the body and blood of Jesus are truly present in the Lord's Supper. I explained to our young people that, yes, we believe this is the true body and blood of Jesus for the forgiveness of sins. However, this is a heavenly meal, not an earthly meal. How this takes place, we leave up to the almighty Son of God. We do not try to explain the chemistry involved in the mystery of the Lord's Supper. We just take Jesus at his word on this matter. Well, our congregation's children were comforted to know that our denomination's high view of the Lord's Supper was in no wise a launching pad for cannibalism.

Anyway, I spoke one day to the very liberal protestant pastor about the cannibalism matter while we were both at the local post office. I politely asked him if what I had heard about his alleged teachings were true, namely, that he was telling his children that we Lutherans were making man-eating a part of our menu. Previously, I was aware that the former professor who was now a pastor had taught that the Bible was a book loaded with errors, contradictions, and mistakes. Therefore, I was not expecting much in the manner of a Biblical answer from him. Still, I wanted to set the record straight that the Lutheran view of the Lord's Supper is not a proof text for eating human flesh.

To my surprise, this former seminary educator said, "Indeed, you Lutherans are cannibals."

Gently, patiently, I tried to explain to him the same truths that my church's children had already grasped, but he was way too huffy and puffy to listen. Curious, I asked him if, in theory, he thought it would be possible for Jesus to be truly present in the Lord's Supper.

"Definitely not!" he exclaimed. "Impossible" he muttered.

Even in theory, he would not grant that Jesus could perform such a task.

So I asked, "Well, you do believe Jesus is the almighty Son of God?"

"Nope," he responded.

"Really!" in amazement, I responded. "Well, you do believe that Jesus rose bodily from the dead, don't you?"

"Nope," he brusquely replied.

"Do your members know you hold these radical beliefs?"

"Nope," he answered.

"Why not, they are fine Christian people, they deserve to know," was my comeback.

"Well, Kurowski, they just have not asked the right questions," he told me.

Having high regard for the members of the congregation that this man was poisoning and low regard for his dishonesty toward the saints, I began to get irked at this wildcat preacher's recklessness.

"Let me ask you," I then said, "What do you preach on Easter?"

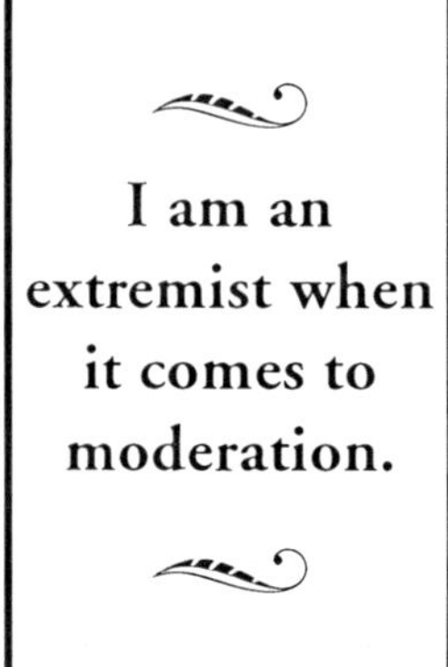

"Well, Kurowski, you fundamentalist, I tell them that Jesus spiritually rose from the dead, and that way I don't bother to preach all of that bodily-resurrection crud!"

Even though I was quite sure that he didn't really know what a fundamentalist was, I was appalled that this charlatan preacher—a 666 ace if I ever saw one—was able to take pleasure in pulling a fast one on his own laity. At the same time, he was swallowing camels—denying the bodily resurrection of Jesus—and straining gnats by making hairsplitting decisions designed to fool people, control people, and manipulate his audience.

Fed up with his hypocrisy, I told this radical minister, "Listen, if we are ever in a public arena and you are leading a prayer, I am going to walk out of the room. The person that your members, my members, and I pray to is the Savior who has risen bodily from the dead. The one you pray to is a figment of your imagination, a dead savior, a dormant deity."

That response did not endear me to this hermeneutical Houdini. I will bend over backwards with fellow Christians, but this man—at least at that moment—was not a Christian. His object of worship was a dead Jesus, not a living Lord. At least in his case, there was no happy inconsistency to save him.[13]

Three, I am an extremist when it comes to moderation. This does not mean I am a moderate. Unfortunately, that formerly good term has developed considerable baggage. Today, being a moderate often means taking a middle-of-the-road position for the sole sake of compromise. The truth of God's Word cannot be dealt with in that fashion. By God's grace, I strive to find the theological golden middle by living within Biblical tensions, taking a paradoxical path, and living with a whole lot of mystery. Lutherans are paradoxical people. That is why our theology will reflect elements of the Baptist heritage, elements of the Roman

Catholic heritage, elements of the Episcopalian heritage, elements of the Presbyterian heritage, and the like. This makes us hard people to peg and pigeonhole. Luther said of himself that he was no fixed star. Therefore, I beg the reader's forbearance.

Fourth, St. Augustine, Blaise Pascal, Martin Luther, C.S. Lewis, and Adolph Köberle have been key theological mentors for my thinking.[14] All five were poets of paradox. Augustine, Pascal, Luther, and Lewis all had three common traits. First, they each were savants who had photographic memories that allowed them to cognitively grasp the whole of Scripture. Under guidance from the Holy Spirit, that ability enabled them to see from Genesis to Revelation the core teachings of Scripture that are the composite of polar opposites. Second, at one time each of these geniuses was either an unbeliever or very angry with God. In other words, they could see reality from the perch of deep doubt, despair, and unbelief as well as deep faith and trust in the triune God. Third, each one had a profound view of the person and work of Jesus Christ. Through the person and work of Jesus, they saw how Christianity was radically set apart from the rest of the religions of the world. These luminaries saw that in the end there are but two religions in the world. The conclusion of Monier-Williams set forth this 180-degree difference between Christianity and the non-Christian religions of the world. In striking words, Williams wrote:

> In the discharge of my duties for forty years as professor of Sanskrit in the University of Oxford, I have devoted as much time as any man living to the study of the sacred books of the East, and I have found the one keynote, the one diapason, so to speak, of all these so-called sacred books, whether it be the Veda of the Brahmans, the Puranas of Siva and Vishnu, the Koran of the Mohammedans, the Zend-Avesta of the Parsees, the Tripitaka of the Buddhists—the one refrain through all—salvation by works. They all say that salvation must be purchased, must be bought with a price, and that the sole price, the sole purchase money, must be our own works and deserving. Our own holy Bible,

> our sacred Book of the East, is from beginning to end a protest against this doctrine. Good works are, indeed, enjoined upon us in that sacred Book of the East far more strongly than in any other sacred book of the East; but they are only the outcome of a grateful heart—they are only a thank-offering, the fruits of faith. They are never the ransom money of the true disciples of Christ. Let us not shut our eyes to what is excellent and true and of good report in these sacred books, but let us teach Hindus, Buddhists, Mohammedans, that there is only one sacred Book of the East that can be their mainstay in that awful hour when they pass all alone in the unseen world. It is the sacred Book which contains that faithful saying, worthy to be received of all men, women, and children, and not merely of us Christians—that Christ Jesus came into the world to save sinners.[15]

Regarding Adoph Köberle, I know little about the biographical details of this erudite evangelical. He wrote his Christian classic *"The Quest for Holiness"*[16] in the crucible of Germany in the 1930s. At this time, an extremist by the name of Adoph Hitler was on the rise. It is my favorite book, next to the Bible. Pascal's *"Pensees,"* C.S. Lewis' *"Mere Christianity,"* Luther's 1535 commentary on Galatians, and Augustine's *"Confessions"* are other books that this paradoxicalist keeps close to his nightstand. These works help pull me out of the ditches of extremism whenever my sinful nature starts sniffing the intoxicating fumes of fanaticism.

Fifth, one may wish to argue that certain paradoxes I advance are not, in fact, paradoxical. Perhaps, you might choose to categorize them as irony instead. That is fine. My goal simply is to sensitize readers to the major paradoxes contained in the Bible and help them see how the Bible is the best message available to thwart extremes.

Sixth, I humbly confess that I am an expert in extremes. I come from a tradition that believes even the best Christian continues to sin in all that he or she does. In fact, we sin in more than all we do when one considers the sin of omission. Thus, from first-hand experience, I know

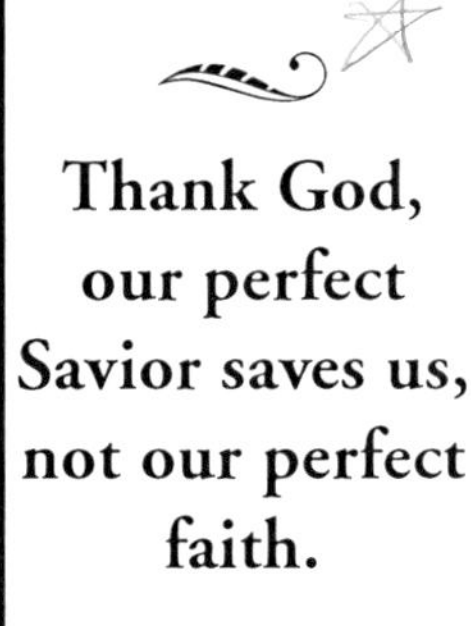

how easy it is to fall into theological ditches. I have tumbled into ditches on the right side of the road. On other occasions, I have found myself mired in the opposite ditch. There were times when I was too narrow and other times when I was too wide in my applications of law and gospel, sin and grace, judgment and pardon. Even after 27 years as a parish pastor, I find myself continually slipping on theological banana peels.

One of our church's finest theologians, an expert on the doctrine of justification, once mentioned to me, "All of us pastors teach false doctrine somewhere along the line."

This becomes acutely problematic when we continually desire to stay in the ditch once someone lovingly points out our location. Again, thank God, our perfect Savior saves us, not our perfect faith.

Oh yes, did you catch the word *lovingly* in the second-to-last line of the prior paragraph? Too swiftly, we witness in the church brothers and sisters who go for the jugular vein of each other. A brother makes a mistake and we pounce on him like a saber-toothed tiger. When that happens, our sinful anger can get in the way. It blocks objectivity. It blinds. It can lead to us straining gnats and swallowing camels. (Galatians 6:1-2)

The opposite extreme is that we are apathetic to the very teachings that cause people to stumble in their faith or prevent people from coming to know Jesus. Luther rightly reminds us that the Holy Spirit is no skeptic. God's Word is the clearest book in the world simply because the Holy Spirit breathes forth its every message. Furthermore, if Jesus—as the cosmic risen Lord of the universe—went through all the trouble of dying on the cross the worst death in history on our behalf, then he is not going to give us a mumbo-jumbo book to guide us through life. The notion that the Bible is unclear runs contrary to the very core and nature of the gospel. In the same breath, we must ask the Holy Spirit to enlighten us.

The brilliant Baptist exegete A.T. Robertson once observed that St. Paul seemed, at times, to write like John Calvin. At other times, Robertson claims that St. Paul writes more like Jacob Arminius. It was his wry way of observing the paradoxical character of divine freedom and human responsibility that is set forth in Scripture. It was Robertson's way of saying we must let God be God. With that observation in mind, let us begin to explore some of the paradoxical riches of Scripture and the thinking pattern of prime time paradoxicalists. It is a good way to limit a measure of swallowing camels and straining gnats. It is a good way to give glory to God and comfort to poor sinners. It is a good way to rejoice in the fact that Jesus perfectly kept the law while he imparts to us through the gospel his perfect record. (Matthew 5:17; 2 Corinthians 5:19-21)

Chapter 3

ELUDING EXTREMES

During May and June of 2000, it was my privilege to attend the forty-seventh National Security Forum at the U.S. Air Force's War College in Montgomery, Ala. During a week of study, debate, plenary forums, and one-on-one discussion, we learned much about National Security threats to our nation. Physicists, Hollywood producers, doctors, lawyers, historians, clergy, and civic leaders from around the nation participated in this think tank conference.

One of the people I met in small group debates between high-ranking military officers and civilians was a lady from Washington, D.C. This martial arts expert had a unique calling. Her job was to protect people from assassination by fanatics on the far right as well as the far left. She told me that she had had 34 clients. She had been able to protect thirty-three of them. A zealot, however, killed one of her clients, when the client failed to properly follow protection protocol.

In our discussions, this lady was very intrigued when I shared with her the paradoxical nature of the Bible. The thesis that the core message of the Bible is one of anti-extremism was especially appealing to her. In particular, she latched hold of the words of a repentant Solomon in Ecclesiastes, chapter seven.

You will recall that Solomon had lived a life of extremes. He was a combination of Martha Stewart, Albert Einstein, Bill Gates, Eero Saarinen, George Washington Carver, Henry Kissinger, Brad Pitt, and Hugh Hefner. Put all the talents and tendencies of those folks into one body with a weakened moral compass and you will get Solomon. Despite all that talent, this man without any mental or moral brakes or balance ended up frittering away most of his life by "chasing the wind." (Ecclesiastes 2) Unfettered from God's Word, Solomon lost his balance stumbling after a life of excesses. Looking back on his days of extreme madness, Solomon took this paradoxical posture:

> Do not be over righteous, neither be over wise—why destroy yourself?
> Do not be over wicked, and do not be a fool—why die before your time?
> It is good to grasp the one and not let go of the other.
> The man who fears God will avoid all extremes.
>
> (Ecclesiastes 7:16-18, New International Version)

Sound evangelical theology takes to heart Solomon's advice. It avoids theological extremes. It seeks at every turn to avoid being too plastic or too elastic. It excises legalism as well as eschews lawlessness. Here Solomon utters a word of law—what we must do—in order to avoid extremes. Similarly, throughout the Hebrew Scriptures and the Greek New Testament, the central message of the Bible cuts a paradoxical path between these extremes—legalism and lawlessness. Chiefly it does this with a message that while salvation does not come by works, nevertheless, it works.

Ultimately, the Spirit's core concern is to identify any spiritual movement that adds to, or subtracts from, the perfect saving work of Jesus, the Messiah. For to chip away at God's greatest gift will always take a person over a cliff. Tension Deficit Disorder of some stripe will set in. A person will become enamored at the possibility of being his or her own god. Either through deeds or through lawless creeds, these individuals will invariably slip into the arms of Lady Legalism or Lady Lawlessness. In turn, this leads to a majoring in minors, swallowing camels and straining gnats.

Roughly twenty centuries ago, St. Paul wrote a beautifully balanced letter to the Christians at Galatia. In this Asia Minor congregation, members were sorely tempted to make a major mistake by following the path of one extremist or the other. In fact, some had already done so. In this heart-on-his-sleeve letter, St. Paul notes how even the apostle Peter, after Pentecost, had slid into one of the dangerous ditches, namely legalism. (Galatians 2:11-16)

In order to keep Christians in that neighborhood from falling over perilous precipices into the chasm of salvation by works (i.e. a salvation that does not work), Paul takes the early church's members on a skillful theological toboggan ride. Staying entirely within the boundaries of the gospel, (Galatians 1:6-9) Paul masterfully shows that the Christian life is a sled ride between self-flattering legalism and self-annihilating lawlessness. (Galatians 5:1-3; 15-16)

In this letter, one also sees how the gospel is paradoxically both inclusive and exclusive. It is inclusive in that Jesus Christ died for all: Jew and Gentile, male and female, slave and free. (Galatians 3:26-29) Through the gift of faith in Jesus and the gifts that Jesus bestows in baptism, God desires all to become Abraham's offspring. However, those who reject this all-inclusive offer will find, as Martin Franzmann writes, how "the all-inclusive gospel of grace excludes all movements and all men (or women) who seek to qualify its grace."[17]

At any given time, a church body as well as an individual Christian will need to live in repentance for failures where there is too wide or too narrow a confession and a practice of God's Word. Wisely, the first of Martin Luther's Ninety-five Theses stated, "When our Lord and Master, Jesus Christ, said, 'Repent ye,' he meant that the whole life of the Christian is one of continual repentance."[18] At the same time, within the Christendom, we must be aware of the fact that most church bodies are losing a sense of their gospel core. This gospel core keeps the church from following the extremes that the remainder of the world is always dishing up.

Reinhold Niebuhr, an outstanding theologian of the old Evangelical and Reformed church, would likely not be at home in his church body today. Even back in 1952, he saw how some were beginning to gut and guillotine the paradoxical nature of the gospel from the church body. He witnessed how the message of the cross was being crossed out and replaced by human activism.[19] Yahweh's redemptive deeds of salvation were being benched in favor of human works as the main trigger to usher in a kingdom of God. Niebuhr lamented how "a God without wrath brought men without sin into a kingdom without judgment through the ministrations of a Christ without a cross."[20]

Without the message of the cross front and center, Christendom will have less and less power to avoid the maddening excesses of this world. It will have no more power than any other religion wherever the message of the cross is not present. On top of this, contemporary Christendom will lack the power of God unto salvation, sanctification, and renewal. Devoid of the peculiar paradoxical perceptive powers that the message of the cross gives, church bodies will depart at the same time from a path of radical grace and theological moderation.[21]

Some years ago, I visited the golden Dome of the Rock shrine in Jerusalem. Under this dome is the alleged rock on which Abraham was supposed to sacrifice his son as a test of faith in God. I was surprised when the Muslim guide at the shrine told me this was where Abraham offered to sacrifice his son Ishmael. I mentioned to him that the Hebrew Scriptures state that it was Abraham's son, Isaac.

He said the Hebrew Scriptures are wrong.

I then declared the Greek Old Testament also reveals it was Isaac, not Ishmael.

Once again, he responded, "The Greek Old Testament is wrong."

I then asked this guide if he believed in the New Testament as a worthy, reliable document.

"Of course," was his instant reply.

"Well, the New Testament, in Hebrews 11, indicates that it also was Isaac."[22]

Without hesitation, the guide did some revision.

"Hebrews 11 is wrong," he announced.

Jesus connects the glory of God with his crucifixion.

When it comes to the Bible, if you pick and choose, you are sure to lose. A form of Attention Deficit Disorder was part of the problem for this well-meaning sentry of the stone. Yet, as I walked away from the alleged spot on Mt. Moriah, it occurred to me that the young man's problem ran much deeper. He had a major case of Tension Deficit Disorder as well as Attention Deficit Disorder. At the core of his unbelief system was the rejection of the glory of God through the profound paradox of the cross. Having rejected this monumental messianic mountaintop, he was simply not open to any other line of reason. Having rejected this paramount paradox, his theology was a gored ox. Having rejected the message of the cross, he really was not interested in the Hebrew Scriptures, the Greek Septuagint, or the New Testament Greek; all of which indicate Isaac and Abraham were the ones who went up to Mt. Moriah. Despite the mouths of three sacred witnesses, the guide preferred a Johnny-come-lately testimony that was utterly at variance with the Hebrew and Greek Scriptures.

It is the cross of Jesus where one sees the brightest revelation of God's love in history. In John 12:23-32, Jesus connects the glory of God with his crucifixion. It is God's strange glory. It was the pattern of Jesus' life. It is to be the template of the life of his disciples. In losing one's life, one gains their life. Ironically, radical Islam falls into both ditches at once when it rejects the paradoxes of the cross. Lawlessly, it destroys innocent life. Legalistically, it advocates salvation by human works. Sadly, this is what can easily happen if we reject God's most magnificent display of love.

At the same time, the message of the cross of Christ is the deepest expression of God's love and the most balancing influence in helping people avoid the seduction of extremes. When properly understood, the message of the cross keeps us from swallowing camels (lawlessness) and straining gnats (legalism). The person who rejects this most profound display of paradoxes that took place on Good Friday will be prone to reject lesser paradoxes, thus making his or her reasoning more brittle, the psyche more bitter, and outlook much bleaker. Let me conclude this chapter with a few of the paradoxes of the cross as a summary of this section and a prelude to the next:

Paradoxes of the Cross

God's severest judgment upon evil, his greatest manifestation of good
The cross: instrument of death and instrument of life
The cross: place of curse and source of blessing
Point of greatest sin and greatest revelation of sinlessness
The eternal God dies
Darkness at noon
Worst day in history, best day in history
Jesus did his most powerful work while he was weakest on the cross
In death, Jesus gives life
Dying man looks to dying Son of Man for life
God is separated from God
The just dies for the unjust
God prays to God
One dies for all
In death, Jesus opens up graves
Life wills to die
Satan succeeds, yet fails
The King of Kings is dead; long live the King of Kings
Miscarriage of justice leads to a decision of "not guilty"
Baptism today connects with a cross that is 2,000 years old

Eluding Extremes

By his stripes we are healed
One malefactor believes, the other does not
Jesus serves as both victim (lamb) and priest
Jesus shepherds his flock by taking on sacrificial role of Lamb of God
Jesus is rejected so that we are accepted
The first becomes last so that the least might become first
Jesus suffers hell while on earth
The cross: severe law and Mt. Everest gospel
The cross: ugly and beautiful
The cross: God revealed and God hidden

Chapter 4

POET OF PARADOX: AN EXAMPLE

The use of paradox to set forth that which is orthodox was an instrument that Martin Luther enlisted throughout his career as a preacher, teacher, and writer. This instrument of communication—paradox—functioned as a tremendous tool for Martin Luther to advance the gospel during the sixteenth century. Moreover, it is no less of a hermeneutical mechanism to convey truth for interpreters of reality who witness the deadly drift of much of Christendom into extremes so far a field from core convictions held throughout the ages.

Throughout his writings, Luther reveals himself not only to be a marvelous teacher of the gospel, but also a poet of paradox. In reality, the two traits go hand in hand. Paradox flows from the gospel because the very nature of the gospel is profound paradox. From the paradoxical message of the cross to God choosing a nation of slaves to bring people freedom, the Bible exudes paradoxes. Once again, the very fact that God declares the ungodly as godly (Romans 4:5) seems like a colossal contradiction of the highest order, yet it is the heart of the gospel.

As with his use of reason, Luther placed paradox under Scripture. For him, it was a servant-tool to help him scale by faith the otherwise insurmountable theological problems and helped him to hurdle what otherwise would be theological pitfalls. In a similar vein, paradox for Luther became a device to help guard against all attempts to explain the mysteries of God to men. For Luther, such egotistical efforts vitiated against the very nature of faith itself. The whole purpose of life is to learn to trust in God. Rationalistic proofs rule out the need to believe, love, and trust. They are an intellectual biting into the fruit of the Tree of Knowledge of Good and Evil. Luther held the Pauline and Augustinian pattern, namely, that believing is seeing. (2 Corinthians 5:7)

From Wittenberg to Heidelberg, from Wartburg to Augsburg, and to the very end of his life, Luther made abundant use of paradox. He saw that although the coin of truth was one, it often had a different imprint on each side. While a host of well-meaning Erasmian theologians in his day overemphasized one truth at the expense of another truth, Luther sought via paradox to hold simultaneously both sides of a given truth, even when the strands seemed to contradict one another.

F. Scott Fitzgerald once said, "The test of a first-rate intelligence is the ability to hold two opposed ideas in the mind at the same time and still retain the ability to function."[23] Martin Luther's first-rate mind and photographic memory no doubt aided him in simultaneously holding two different sides of the truth. While these superb natural gifts of mind from God assisted Luther in becoming a poet of paradox, above all, the Holy Spirit revealed to him a plethora of paradoxical truths that were the most powerful forces in the Reformation.

The fact that paradox, for Luther, was not a gain by man's brain sets Luther apart from ancient poets of paradox. It was God's good grace rather than man's good head that was the source of sound paradoxical expression. Unlike the ancients who saw paradox as a rhetorical device to solve the enigma with some rationalistic synthesis, Luther used paradox to confess the double-edged sword truths of God's revealed mysteries.

A place where one can see the early Luther making vigorous use of paradox is Heidelberg. It was about a half-year after Luther had posted his Ninety-five Theses on October 31, 1517, on the north door of the Castle Church at Wittenberg, a sort of bulletin board for the

The church fathers were, for Luther, a good check and balance to his teachings

university. Controversy swamped the disputation that Luther hoped would occur after posting his Ninety-five Theses: smashing to pieces the practice of indulgences. Johann von Staupitz, vicar of Luther's Augustinian order, counseled Luther not to debate controversial subjects that attacked the financial Fugger-fueled forgiveness of Tetzel and Leo X. Instead, Staupitz enjoined Luther to prepare disputation theses that would treat subjects such as free will, sin, and grace.

Keep in mind that the Church of Rome, at this time, was suffering from major Tension Deficit Disorder. On numerous levels, the church slipped into extremism. First, the church hierarchy was putting a price on the gift of forgiveness of sins that Jesus merited upon the cross. Here, Lady Lawlessness and Lady Legalism had seduced it at the same time. Second, for some time the church was willing to put to death people who disagreed with papal leaders. John Hus was burned at the stake 100 years earlier in his attempt to bring the Church of Rome back to the Bible. Jesus had never given the church this kind of temporal authority—to put people to death. On the contrary, Jesus rebuked the apostle Peter in the garden of Gethsemane when Peter used his sword to lop off the ear of Malchus, servant of the high priest.[24]

The last thing on Luther's mind was to start any new church body. He was simply a pious monk who wanted the church to go back to its rich paradoxical gospel heritage. In addition to being a very good exegete and one outstanding systematician, one who could integrate the whole of Scripture, Luther was a top-flight historian. He knew very well what the early church fathers taught. He studied them carefully, especially Augustine. The church fathers were, for Luther, a good check and balance to his teachings. He did not want to usher new, dubious, Johnny-come-lately teachings into the church. He wanted to be historical, not hysterical, when it came to being in step with the Scripture-taught traditions of the church.

With courage, clarity, and courtesy, Luther prepared and presented twenty-eight theological and twelve philosophical theses for his Heidelberg disputation. In addition, he formulated short Biblical proofs for the theological theses. Right from the beginning, Luther prepares his fellow monks to hear a presentation of his new, yet old, evangelical theology in the form of paradoxes:

> Distrusting completely our own wisdom, according to the counsel of the Holy Spirit, "Do not rely on our own insight," [Proverbs 3:5] we humbly present to the judgment of all those who wish to be here these theological paradoxes, so that it may become clear whether they have been deduced well or poorly from St. Paul, the especially chosen vessel and instrument of Christ, and also from St. Augustine, his most trustworthy interpreter.[25]

Early in his disputation, Luther began to fulfill his promise to present paradoxes. Paradox wrapped the very first theological thesis he set forth. He asserted how God's good law led to bad results.[26] Although God's law is in itself a good tonic, in a fallen world the law led to toxic results. Wrote Luther, "The law of God, the most salutary doctrine of life, cannot advance man on his way of righteousness, but rather hinders him."[27]

In theses three and four, Luther shows that what most often is beautiful to man is ghastly to God; and, that God holds in high regard what man often holds in low esteem. What Luther did is prepare the way for assertions relevant to the theology of the cross. Theses three and four read this way:

3. Although the works of man always seem attractive and good, they are nevertheless likely to be mortal sins.
4. Although the works of God are always unattractive and appear evil, they are nevertheless really eternal merits.[28]

Luther's paradoxical progression toward the cross culminates in a contrast between two different theologies: the theology of glory versus the theology of the cross. The theology of glory proposes to perceive the invisible things of God through the visible things of life. Luther labels such a theology as bankrupt; it attacks faith and therefore assaults grace. In Luther's estimate, the person who looks to find God via an evidential or empirical theology does not deserve the title of theologian. Vigorously Luther charges, "A theology of glory calls evil good and good evil. A theology of the cross calls the thing what it actually is."[29]

As a whole, the 28 theses of Luther's Heidelberg disputation cut with a sharp paradoxical edge. Two more examples will further show this to be the case. First, on the subject of grace, Luther's Janusian-like approach issues another paradox. Wrote Luther, "It is certain that a man must utterly despair of his own ability before he is prepared to receive the grace of Christ."[30] While St. Paul is the prime tributary to Luther's wellspring of paradoxes, here one sees the reformer drawing from our Lord's Sermon on the Mount. (Matthew 5:3)

Second, thesis 26 of the Heidelberg disputation reveals the paradoxical polarities of law and gospel. By means of these two handles, law and gospel, Luther gained a hermeneutical hold of what otherwise might be viewed as seemingly slippery contradictions. The law says what we do saves us (Matthew 19:17) while the gospel says what Jesus did saves us. (Galatians 3:13, 26) Which one is it? Is Scripture giving two opposite answers to life's answers to life's major question? Do we have here polar positions unable to be reconciled? In thesis 26, Luther's good grasp of the law-gospel dialectic shows how God bridges the gap. Luther asserts, "The law says, 'do this,' and it is never done. Grace says 'believe in this,' and everything is already done."[31]

Before closing commentary on the Heidelberg disputation, we must note one more striking paradox alluded to by Luther in a presentation to fellow Augustinians at a general meeting in Heidelberg. It is one of his most famous paradoxes. Profound. Comforting. Penetrating. Liberating. Comprehensive. The words of this paradox sketch the picture of the ever renewed struggle between sin and grace, the natural man and the new man in Christ, the old Adam and the new Adam in the believer. What is this paradox? It is that Christians are, at the same time, both sinner and saint.[32, 33]

The truth that the Christian, standing before God, is at the same time just and a notorious sinner was an indissoluble reality of existence that Luther could set forth only by way of paradox. It enabled Luther to see that every Christian is a living paradox. It enabled Luther to see that, at least in the context of faith, while man resides in a fallen world then this paradox also arises: only a divided person is a whole person. Luther did not try to dissolve this point of tension, as Hegel would have done. Dr. Martin Scharlemann summarizes Luther's paradoxical posture that is embraced in the succinct formula "simultaneously sinner and saint" in this fashion:

> As the Reformer discovered from his serious study of the Bible and from the anguish of the soul, this situation is sketched neither in terms of legal fiction nor of a pious hope—either of which would help solve the contradiction—but as a present and dependable fact. He found that as a person, in relationship to God, the ultimate dimension of life, he had to think of God's utter rejection of him and His gracious acceptance of him as an indissoluble unity of existence.[34]

As a living paradox, it made good Biblical sense to Luther that paradox permeates a Christian's whole way of looking at things.[35] For example, Luther saw how the prayer life of a Christian is also paradoxical. In a sermon on prayer and life given during the year 1519, Luther linked prayer and paradox. He wrote, "We pray after all because we are not worthy to pray."[36] To a mind that is captive under the law, this makes no sense whatsoever; it is another seeming contradiction. To a mind under the gospel, by way of paradox, Luther saw how Christians become, as Dr. Francis Rossow put it, "worthy unworthies."[37]

In his 1520 tract, *The Freedom of the Christian*, Luther set forth another monumental paradox. In this tract, he demonstrated how God's justifying grace liberated the sinner who had been a slave of sin to become a slave of righteousness. Leaning upon the apostles Peter and Paul, Luther saw how walking in freedom meant walking in service. In describing the liberty that Christians have, Luther put the essence of the matter in two apparently opposite propositions: "The Christian is a perfectly free lord of all, subject to none. A Christian is a perfectly dutiful servant of all, subject to all."[38]

In formulating this paradox, Luther assails legalism as well as assaults license. Sweaty realist that he was, Luther holds in tension the freedom that comes from justification before God and the responsibility we have as those redeemed living in Christ's kingdom. For Luther, this axiom of freedom through slavery was another way of expressing the inextricable link between justification and sanctification. By this paradox, Luther avoids a synergistic solution to justification and an antinomian characterization of sanctification. It was another way of declaring that faith and works are like fire and heat. It was also, at the same time, another way of saying: while good works are not necessary for salvation, they are necessary. In so formulating this paradox, Luther avoided the extremes of either Lady Legalism or Lady Lawlessness.

Luther's penchant for paradox shows up continuously in his writings. In 1521, he wrote *Comfort When Facing Grave Temptations*, in which he asserts that the worst trial in life is to have no trial at all.[39] Trials under the gospel stir up the faith. The worst thing that could happen to one in life is to have no trial at all and conclude that he or she did not need God. Luther, like the Psalmist, strongly believed that a measure of trial was crucial to the alchemy of faith. (Psalm 119:67) Upon the study of this Psalm, Luther stated that God has given us a holy trio to fight: the devil, the world, and our sinful flesh. Through trial, through meditation upon God's Word and Christ's love, and through prayer, God enables us to fight the devil, the world, and our sinful flesh.

Luther's commentary on the Magnificat contains an especially eloquent use of paradox. Often God works in strange, hidden, and unexpected ways. Adroitly, Luther affirms this:

> Even so, Christ was powerless on the cross; and yet there He performed His mightiest work and conquered sin, death, world, hell, Devil, and all evil. Thus all the martyrs were strong and overcame.[39]

Later, Luther writes:

> Who is like the Lord, our God, who is seated high, who looks far down upon the heavens and the earth? For since He is the Most High, and yet there is nothing above Him, He cannot look above Him, nor yet to either side, for there is none like Him. He must needs, therefore, look within Him and beneath Him; and the farther one is beneath Him, the better does He see him.[40]

In 1525, the rapier one-dimensional wit of Eramus' legalistic pen met the paradoxical dual exhaust of Luther's gospel-powered quill. Martin Luther's *The Bondage of the Will* was quite likely a lot more than Erasmus bargained for. The humanist from Rotterdam had drawn first blood against Luther with *The Freedom of the Will.* Vigorously, with polemics in one hand and paradoxes in the other, Luther admonished Erasmus for his aversion to paradoxes. For Luther, much of Erasmus' problem resided in his inability to distinguish between paradoxes and contradictions. Because Erasmus mistakes the latter for the former, he concludes that the Scriptures are obscure. This is a seduction by the prince of darkness! With biting irony, Luther asks the humanist who it is that thinks the Holy Spirit speaks with forked tongue:

> My dear Erasmus, let me say in turn: If you think these paradoxes are inventions of men, what are you contending about? Why are you so roused?... If, therefore, God has willed that such things [paradoxes] should be openly spoken of and published abroad without regard to consequences, who are we to forbid it?[41]

Plainly, one sees Luther's view on the propagation of paradoxes. Proclaim them. Publish them. Pronounce them. Furthermore, do not measure them by the judgment of finite, fallen man. In fact, paradoxes are crucial to the whole element of faith in that the hidden quality of them calls for trust, not unbelief. Who needs trust if one can rationalistically explain the mysteries of faith? Taking aim at all theologians of glory who, like Erasmus, want to walk by sight rather than faith, Luther strings together a series of paradoxes showing them as an instrument of faith as well as a way to confess the one true faith. Luther continues:

> Hence in order that there be room for faith, it is necessary that everything which is believed should be hidden. However, it cannot be more deeply hidden than under an object, perception, or experience that is contrary to it. Thus when God makes alive He does it by killing, when He justifies He does it by making men guilty, when He exalts to heaven He does it by bringing down to hell, as Scripture says: "The Lord kills and brings to life; He brings down to Sheol and raises up." (1 Samuel 2:6)[42]

Luther sees Erasmus' aversion to Scriptural paradoxes as a misguided attempt not to let God be God.[43] Erasmus cannot hold simultaneously the hot, tough, tandem truths of Scripture that Luther picks up by faith with the tongs of paradox. While Erasmus recoils from the clearly revealed truth of God hardening hearts, unable to line it up with the love of God, Luther simultaneously grips both truths of God's inscrutable ways through this paradoxical assertion: "As far as God is concerned, therefore, he does nothing but harden by continual goodness and nothing but show mercy by continual punishment."[44]

Luther never stopped using paradoxes to confess the faith. In his 1535 commentary on Galatians, Luther openly exclaimed how the law-gospel paradox "knocks out the teeth of the law."[45] In explaining his hermeneutic, Luther declared, "This is our theology; and when it is said that I am not only blind and deaf to the law and free from it but completely dead to it, these are paradoxes strange to reason and absurd."[46] Shortly after that assertion, Luther presents this paradox about death, "Death, you have nothing on me. For I have another death, one that kills you, my death. And the death that kills is stronger than the death that is killed."[47]

Poet of Paradox: An Example

In a grand flare of the use of paradox, Luther confesses how God uses the law, sin, and death to defeat the law, sin, and death. His theology of opposites sparkles with this paradoxical paragraph:

> Thus with the sweetest names Christ is called my law, my sin, and my death, in opposition to the law, sin, and death, even though in fact He is nothing but sheer liberty, righteousness, life, and eternal salvation. Therefore He became law to the law, sin to sin, and death to death, in order that He might redeem me from the curse of the law, justify me, and make me alive. And so Christ is both; while He is the law, He is liberty; while He is sin, He is righteousness; and while He is death, He is life. For by the very fact that He permitted the law to accuse Him, sin to damn Him, and death to devour Him, He abrogated the law, damned sin, and destroyed death, and justified and saved me. Thus, Christ is a poison against the law, sin, and death, and simultaneously a remedy to regain liberty, righteousness, and eternal life.[48]

Even in his serious/playful moments Luther spun paradoxical responses cutting through issues with the double-edge sword of the Spirit.[49] An example of this is his response to a question about the validity of astrology. Luther lived during the early part of the Nostradamus century during which people died early, disaster occurred frequently, and the stars spooked people. Not a few intellectuals bought into astrology then, even as many do today. When someone asked Luther if he believed in astrology, he simply said, "Jacob and Esau!" These two twins of Isaac were born under the same star and the same sign on the same day but went entirely different directions. (Genesis 25:23-28) In Luther's mind, as well as in Isaiah's mind, (Isaiah 47:13-14) astrology was bunk.

During the last ten years of his life, Luther delivered his final set of lectures. His eight-volume set of *Lectures on Genesis* shows Luther as a lover of paradox to the end of his life. In the early portions of the eighth and final volume of his Genesis lectures, Luther's pen pours out one paradox after another. Twice he quotes the paradoxical, prophetic word of 1 Samuel

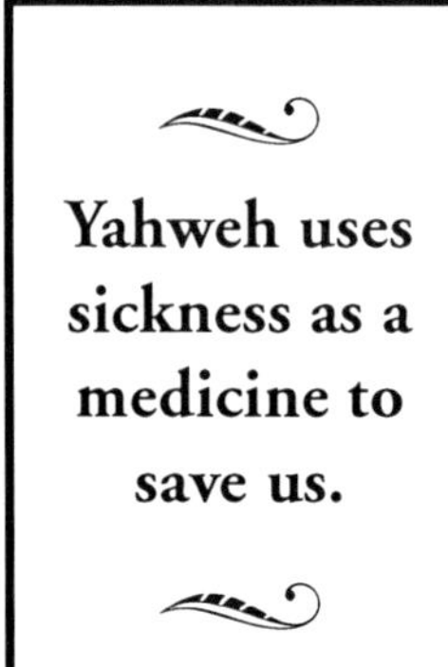

2:6-7, "I kill and bring to life; I bring down to Sheol and raise up; I make poor and make rich."[50] Through the paradoxical spectacles of this Scripture, Luther sees how Yahweh uses sickness as a medicine to save us.[51]

Through the lenses of paradox, Luther sees the hidden God at work. For Luther, paradox becomes a tool—in, with, and under the gospel—for the sixth sense of faith to arise. Through the miracle of baptism and the sure word of God, such faith takes its stand.[52] With high homiletical skill, Luther harvests the story of the Old Testament patriarch, Joseph. In particular, Luther dissects the phrase, "I am Joseph," to show how God took this son of Jacob along the paradoxical path—from dungeons to diadems—in order to make a seasoned saint. Luther describes the paradoxical pattern that God uses as potter to sculpture Joseph:

> "Besides, He is the kind of God who not only makes everything out of nothing but makes nothing out of everything, just as He reduced Joseph to nothing. And when it seemed that Joseph was ruined and lost, He makes everything out of him, that is, the greatest man in the world. But Joseph, on the other hand, divests himself of all rank and game, descends from his royal throne to the lowliest men, his father and brothers, and says: 'I am Joseph.' Here he is again brought down to nothing and is the very Joseph who was cast into the pit, sold, and consigned to slavery. Once more, he becomes the son of a shepherd and says: 'I am your brother, the son of a shepherd, just as you are.' "[53]

Well into the last lectures of his life on Genesis, Luther makes a curious remark. He says, "No one can prevent God from doing things differently."[54] Once more, the vocabulary of faith and paradox are at work. The use of paradox in matters of faith is acknowledging that, from our point of view, God does things differently than what we would expect. Through the gift of faith, God grants us a paradoxical vision to see his unexpected works, ways, and wonders. Above all, Luther enables us to see the paradoxical path of that teaching which is the center of the Scripture: the gospel.[55] At the end of his life, this poet of paradox, Martin Luther, declares, "Before the world Christ is killed, condemned, and descends into hell. But before God this is the salvation of the world from beginning all the way to the end."[56]

The American Luther scholar Donald Mackenzie wrote,

> "Not until Luther came, do we find anyone who can be classified with Augustine for the wealth and depth of his insight into the paradoxical subtlety of the nature of man and the manifold wisdom of God's activity both in nature and redemption."[57]

Although Luther, at times, gave himself over to volcanic eruptions that, for some, overshadowed the depth of his insight into the gospel, nevertheless, his paradoxical approach toward theology is where the church can find compass, rudder, and sails. It is also a rich resource to find insight for a good measure of grace to avoid swallowing camels and straining gnats.

Luther understood that his paradoxical views were controversial. He wrote, 'Thus, by the grace of God, we are holy apostates."[58] He recognized a theology of the cross that engendered attacks from all sides even though it was God's greatest display of love. For the legalist, the cross destroys the illusion that we can do something apart from God thus rendering God less than almighty. For the person bent on lawlessness, the cross says "look how awful all lawlessness is that the holy Son of God must suffer so for the sin of mankind!" With the deepest of convictions, Luther believed this message alone could bring about the needed changes in the church, in culture, and in individual lives. Nothing has changed. Only through a paradoxical vision from a meaty, mighty, majestic gospel can the love of the absolute paradox, Jesus Christ, keep societies from being seduced by the self-centered, self-flattering nudity of Lady Legalism and Lady Lawlessness; the poster prostitutes of secularism.

Chapter 5

The Paradoxical Thread Throughout Scripture

From the opening verses of Sacred Scripture in Genesis to the end of the last chapter of the Apocalypse of John, the Holy Spirit cuts a paradoxical path. The first verse of Scripture reveals the God who stands outside of time speaking of a beginning. (Genesis 1:1) The second-to-last verse of the Bible presents an apostle praying that Emmanuel who is already here (Matthew 28:20) will come soon. (Revelation 22:20)

The paradoxical thread, like the redemptive thread, runs through the Scriptures from cover to cover. The Spirit, like an ever-present, non-stop sewing machine, stitches a tapestry that reminds us that God's gown is infinitely larger than our toga. I believe it was Robert Coleman who said that if God were to try to explain to us the simplest mysteries of the universe, it would be like Albert Einstein trying to explain to a rock-neck crab the theory of relativity.

Let's face it; God's thoughts are not our thoughts. His ways are not our ways; and his judgments are unsearchable, unfathomable, and unbelievable—except as the Holy Spirit calls us by the gospel. (2 Thessalonians 2:14)[59] Frankly, it should make sense that a good deal of the Bible does not make sense lest there be no need for faith. Also, keep in mind that while the Bible gives us everything we need to know, it is but a trillionth of what we will know once we meet God face to face. Then we will have advanced microchips in our glorified brains to grasp what now is far beyond our finite, fallen reach. Then, sin will not blind us, the world will not seduce us, nor will the devil tempt us.

There is a huge temptation for humans to construct dinky deities, pint-sized pitiful gods that one can walk around like a Chihuahua on a leash. That is part of the flight from paradox. We want boring one-dimensional gods that we can either control by a system of salvation by works or gods that we can tell to go fly a kite as we live like prodigal sons and daughters. For starters, we need to remember that God is not bound to the natural rules he created to run this universe, neither is he bound to dealing with us in ways that are limited to our own finiteness. From the parting of the Red Sea (Exodus 14:21-31) to the causing of the sun to stand still (Joshua 10:12-24) to Jesus ascending into the clouds, (Acts 1:9-11) the universe bows to its Lord.

That there is a surprising amount of paradox in Scripture should come as no surprise to followers of the Lord Jesus. Why? Because paradox always carries with it the aroma of mystery; and what are Christians but "stewards of the mysteries of God." (1 Corinthians 4:1) St. Paul, in describing the nature of faith to Timothy, put it this way, "holding the mystery of the faith in a pure conscience." (1Timothy 3:9)

Through paradox, the eyes of faith see two worlds at work simultaneously. Whether the temporal or eternal, the seen or unseen, the kingdom of Caesar or the kingdom of God, tension points exist that seem contradictory but in fact are not, for with God all things are possible. (Genesis 18:14; Matthew 19:26) The gist of this paradox is this: it is the tension points of paradox that help us cope with the tension points of life. (2 Corinthians 4:8-12)

The apostle Paul wrote to the Corinthians, "For we walk by faith, not by sight." (2 Corinthians 5:7) The thesis of this chapter is that the life of faith in Christ is a life whereby Christians constantly embrace paradoxes, seeing beyond what looks to be a contradiction to beholding deep truths that explain God's mighty acts of creation, redemption, and sanctification. So that our faith might not rest upon human ingenuity, human powers of the mind, or human effort, but rather God's power, God gives us paradoxes, the gospel itself being the chief paradox. This paradox of God declaring the ungodly as godly for the sake of the risen Christ, Paul says is of first importance. (1 Corinthians 15:3) Why? It is the paradox by which we are saved and by which the radical love of God breaks into time and space. (1 Corinthians 15:2; 1 Corinthians 13; 1 Corinthians 3:11)

As we begin a journey of examining a good number of paradoxes in both the Old Testament and the New Testament, we must keep two things in mind. First, the recognition of paradoxes of faith is a gift from God through the work of the Holy Spirit (1 Corinthians 2:10-16) through the good news of Jesus' love. (2 Thessalonians 2:14) Second, by the grace of God, we examine these paradoxes from the Old Testament and New Testament to sharpen our skills in order to cut through the issues confronting the existence of civilization and the seduction of contra-civilization extremes.

Chapter 6

Old Testament Paradoxes

The very first verse of the Old Testament, Genesis 1:1, reverberates with paradoxical echoes: "In the beginning, God created the heavens and the earth." The thought of juxtaposing the eternal God, (Psalm 90:1,2) whose reach is before and beyond time, (2 Peter 3:8) alongside "in the beginning" is the marriage of the Timeless One to the ones of time. In creation we have the intersection of time and eternity by way of a paradox from God who himself is a paradox. The changeless God (Malachi 3:6) brings about change.

How intriguing it is that the first time the Hebrew Scriptures mention God's name, it comes to us in a plural form (*Elohim*), yet we know that God is one. (Deuteronomy 6:4; 1 Corinthians 8:4) As the Hebrew scholar Leupold rightly observes, the term *Elohim* allows for the fuller unfolding of the doctrine of the Trinity. He writes, "Consequently, he who would claim that the term can have no connection with the truth of the Holy Trinity goes too far."[60] Martin Luther, who also excelled in the Hebrew language, draws a similar but bolder conclusion, "But we have clear testimony that Moses aimed to indicate the Trinity or the three persons in the one divine nature."[61]

Later in the chapter, Trinitarian sounds arise again. In Genesis 1:26, God says, "Let us make in our image." Once again, there is a paradoxical movement. Once again, the Spirit reveals that God is at the same time a God of unity, plurality, and mystery. Fuller revelation from Scripture, of course, reveals explicitly what is implicit in the first chapter of Genesis, namely, the truth of God's one divine essence and three distinct persons. (Matthew 28:19) St. Augustine declared that the very truth that God is love implies that within the one divine essence would be a plurality of persons from whom this love flows back and forth.

The inaugural chapter of Genesis contains other paradoxical imprints. The fact that God creates (*bara*) everything out of nothing, (Genesis 1:1) so that things we can see are made out of things that we cannot see (Hebrews 11:3) has a distinct paradoxical ring. Such a revelation enables Christians not to be intimated by small pond scientists who boast about how one day human beings will be able to create life. To create life in the Biblical sense, one must make something out of nothing.

Back in 1970, I attended Oshkosh State University for a year. The head of the religion department back then was an atheist. Vividly I recall how he asserted that human beings would one day be able to create life. Had the professor said make life or produce life, he would have been on safer ground. Blind to the Hebrew concept of *bara*, he slid into the ditch of hubris.

Once one grasps that the God of the Scriptures is a God of omnipotence, this changes everything. It frees one from having to think in superficial one-dimensional terms. For example, so many people stumble over the fact that Jonah was swallowed in the belly of a fish. Even for many Christians this is a logistical problem. If the God who made everything out of nothing wanted to do so, he could put our whole solar system in the belly of the same fish in which Jonah resided for three days and three nights. Part of the charm of the story of Jonah is that God constructs a strange scenario that would be immensely memorable to oral cultures that for ages would not have access to the printed word. And at the heart of this story is the good news of how God so loved the world.

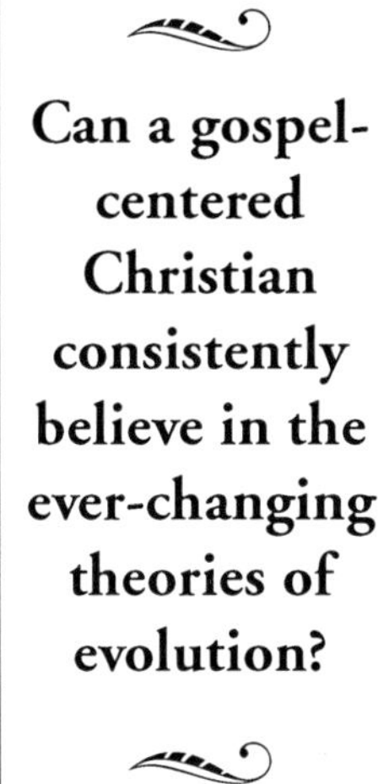

Once a person grasps, through the eyes of faith, the omnipotence of the Redeemer God, you can ride easy in the theological saddle without falling off the horse. You do not become so prone to the dyslectic: putting God into little doghouses. One is able to draw large camels through the eyes of very small needle heads. You even can gain a sense of wonder, imagination, awe, and humor when you consider gigantic issues. You can smile broadly when you read that God called into existence light before he created the luminaries. (Genesis 1:3 cf., 1:14-18) To people who want to put God in a box, this will seem like nonsense. Nevertheless, faith sees what appears to be a contradiction to our finite minds. It beholds the powerful paradoxical patterns of the Creator-Savior.

Such a worldview enables one to take many of the questions pertaining to evolution in stride. Can a gospel-centered Christian consistently believe in the ever-changing theories of evolution? Paradox under the gospel works with awesome assumptions. It recognizes that Jesus is the cosmic mind of the universe come into the flesh and neither bound by time nor space. This disposition of the Holy Spirit permits Christians to live within all kinds of delightful tensions. (Colossians 1:15-20) It provides plenty of room for microevolution whereby people are often speaking really about the adaptation of species to an environment. However, gospel-centered Christians are very suspicious about a host of macroevolution hypotheses. Not only from a Scriptural point of view, but also from a scientific view, the dubious contemporary theories frequently go against known laws of science, lack fossil support, and make all kinds of unproven assumptions. If people want to teach varieties of macroevolution as a theory, most Christians have no problem with that happening. When science mixes with all kinds of philosophical drivel, Christians usually say, "Let's stick to science!"

The biggest problem with macroevolution hypotheses is that most imply that God is responsible for sin and death. If that is the case, then you have a holy God doing unholy things. You slip from paradox to oxymoron. Hitler, Mao, Stalin, and a host of madmen went that direction and the world has still not recovered from their madness. It was Darwin, by the way, who caused Stalin to go off the deep end. Stalin, in turn, became the main philosophical mentor for Saddam Hussein. Today, the extremist thought police would not allow some of the greatest design scientists of the past such as Einstein and Newton to teach in many American classrooms. Left-wing McCarthyism is alive and well today just as is sectarian right-wing fundamentalism that wants to teach a particular brand of creationism under the guise of intelligent design. Really, it should be no big deal to present all views in American classrooms, but neither as a propagandist for any left-wing philosophy nor for any right-wing ideology.

The drumbeat that the gospel's nature is highly paradoxical was present from the very beginning. Immediately in Genesis 3, the story of the fall of mankind into sin revealed a paradoxical twist. Adam and Eve's aspirations to be gods (seeking evolution big time) led them to what Gerhard Forde has termed: "The Upward Fall." Writes Forde:

> The fall is really not what the word implies at all. It is not a downward plunge to some lower level in the great chain of being, some lower rung on the ladder of morality and freedom. Further, it is an upward rebellion, an invasion of the realm of things "above," the usurping of divine prerogative.[62]

This upward fall meets with God's downward ascent. The first gospel promise of the Bible is how God begins in time and space to reverse the upward fall. This promise exudes paradox (Genesis 3:15). We call this good news promise the *Protoevangelium*, which literally means "*the first gospel.*" And not only does it light up with paradox, but it casts a light that will little by little become more brilliant with new rays of revelation as time goes on. In this first gospel promise, God foretells of a rescue mission. He predicts how a savior would gain victory through defeat. Even though the heel of the warrior descendant of Eve will be badly bruised, nevertheless, victory over the devil-serpent deceiver will be obtained.

At the end of the chapter that narrates the fall of Adam and Eve into sin, another paradox quickly falls on the heels of Genesis 3:15. God, in mercy, must keep Adam and Eve from eating from the Tree of Life. He must allow them to die so that they might live. (Genesis 3:22-24) Had they eaten from that tree which had power to impart imperishable physical life, they would have endured more thorns, more thistles, and endless entropy, a nightmare death that would never end. In compassion, God took away the Tree of Life so that they might fully taste the fruit of the eternal Tree of Life through the Lord of life who would hang on a tree of death for them in the fullness of time.

Noah saw the paradoxical hand of the Lord when God used water to destroy an evil world, yet used the same water to save the remnant. (Genesis 7; 1 Peter 3:21) Hence, this worldwide deluge was both a life-taking and life-giving flood. Hundreds of years later, God would repeat this law-gospel water event of paradoxical proportions when the Red Sea became both an instrument of death and life at the same time. (Exodus 14:21-31)

Abraham also saw the paradoxical ways of the Lord when he and Sarah were given a child. From a dead womb, Sarah gave birth to their child, Isaac. (Genesis 18:11-13) Moreover, God's paradoxical command to Abraham to kill his only son, Isaac, seemed to contradict everything that God had earlier promised to Abraham. (Genesis 15:3,4) Still, Abraham used paradox to contend with paradox, believing that even if Isaac died; yet, Isaac would live. (Hebrews 11:19)

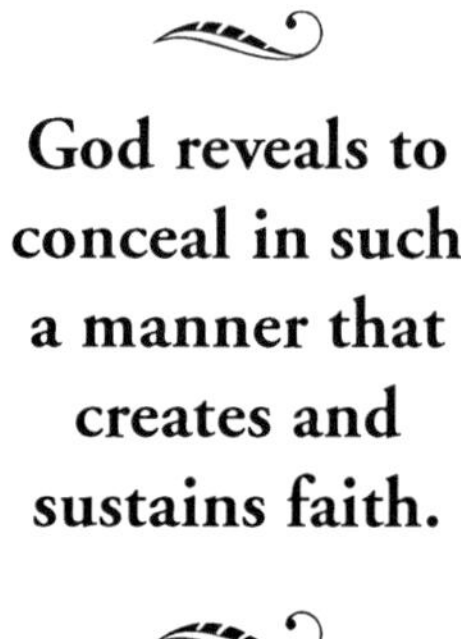

I have picked out only a few examples of paradoxical movement in the book of Genesis to illustrate the use of this tool by the Holy Spirit. As one culls paradoxes from the Hebrew Bible, these examples multiply many times over. Throughout the Bible, a constant tension enjoins believers to avoid legalism and lawlessness, straining gnats and swallowing camels. Even though this is a huge pattern in the Bible, every hermeneutic book I have read has either ignored it or given it little attention.

This work is a pump primer for future works of theology to make more room for paradox as a key interpretive tool. For the purposes of this book, selectivity will be necessary. In this light, several key paradoxes deserve special attention as they relate to the central message of Scripture. One example is the coming of a Savior in the fullness of time to make atonement for the sin of the world.

A key part of God's redemptive plan was to create a kingdom whereby the Creator-Redeemer would go about the matter of re-establishing his rule of grace over men. The choice of the nation to be the vessel that receives the Savior of the world is a prelude to the New Testament paradox, "and the last shall be first." (Matthew 19:30) God would take a nation of slaves to be the nation that freed the world from the slavery of sin. From his storehouse of grace, God would pick the lowliest and least of all peoples—an incarcerated nation—to be the first and foremost of peoples; a nation from which the Magna Charta of Christian liberty would arise. (Deuteronomy 7:6-8a; Galatians 5:1)

One sees Yahweh's paradoxical ways in creating his kingdom throughout the Pentateuch, the first five books of the Bible. From the bush that burns but does not burn up (Exodus 3: 4-22) to a mysterious person who is both an angel and Lord, (Numbers 22:21-35) who is a human being and Lord, (Genesis 18:2-3) a consistent string of paradoxical moves and messengers show up. All along the way, God reveals to conceal in such a manner that creates and sustains faith.

Exodus 33 is a chapter of Scripture that reveals God's hiddenness. On the one hand, it is said that, "And Yahweh spoke to Moses face to face, as a man speaks to his friend." (Exodus 33:11) On the other hand, in the same chapter, when Moses asks God to see his face so that his people will have added assurance for their journey ahead, God says, "Thou canst not see my face: for there shall no man see me, and live." (Exodus 33:20) Through this paradox, we see that "there is a sense in which Israel both sees and does not see the face of Yahweh … so God remains hidden even in the midst of His revelation."[62]

One of the outstanding paradoxes in the Old Testament, a paradox which prepares us for an apex paradox in the New Testament, (Matthew 22:41-45) comes from a Psalm that is quoted more frequently in the New Testament than any other. Psalm 110:1 reads, "The Lord (*Yahweh*) says in reference to my Lord (*Adonai*): 'Sit at my right hand, until I make your enemies your footstool.' "[64] Here is inter-Trinitarian dialogue taking place with God the Father speaking to the Messiah as Priest-King as the Holy Spirit listens and records. Here we see the paradoxical nature of God, one of unity of essence and plurality of persons.

The pinnacle of paradox in the Old Testament comes from Isaiah. The prophet known as the Fifth Evangelist soars on the two wings of paradox. Beginning with his prophecy of the virgin birth and Immanuel's incarnation, the absolute paradox, Isaiah takes flight to lofty levels. Then, another major majestic messianic announcement! The Spirit reveals that wonder-Child would at the same time be the "Mighty God, the Everlasting Father." (Isaiah 9:6) The third piece of royal revelation intensifies the first and second even more. Next we are told this Messiah, both God and man at the same time, would also be the suffering servant who would become the substitutionary sacrifice for the sins of all mankind. (53:4-6) His calling would be what C.S. Lewis terms "against the world, for the world" manifesting the "two-edged character" of the Christian faith.[65]

If we miss these paradoxes regarding the person and work of the promised Messiah, we miss the heart of the gospel that is also the central message of the Old and New Testaments. Once, I read the 53rd chapter of Isaiah to a Jewish lady. She became distressed upon my reading of this chapter and told me bluntly, "Stop reading to me your New Testament." When I gently tried to tell her I was reading the Hebrew Bible she refused to listen and refused to look at the 53rd chapter of Isaiah.[66]

This gospel trail of gospel facets in Isaiah contributes to the grand paradox of the Old Testament! What is this paradox? It is this: the coming Messiah would at the same time be a conquering king (2 Samuel 7:12-16) as well as the suffering servant who would be the great Yom Kippur sacrifice for the sins of the world. (Isaiah 53) Mysteriously, paradoxically, and divinely, the messianic God-man, born of the virgin, would establish an everlasting kingdom (2 Samuel 7:13) through the paradoxical pattern of death and resurrection. (Isaiah 53:8-11)

Unfortunately, few believed the paradoxically staggering prediction that the Messiah would suffer and die for the world's sins, then rise from the dead. In the opening verse of the suffering servant chapter, Isaiah predicted, by way of a rhetorical question, that only a remnant would believe this mountain top messianic paradox. "Who hath believed our report?" (Isaiah 53:1) is the lead into this passion narrative chapter, a chapter that has puzzled so many people in the past. You recall that this chapter puzzled the treasurer from Ethiopia until he heard the good news of Jesus from Philip, the evangelist. (Acts 8:27-39) In addition, more New Testament writers quote this chapter than any other in Hebrew Scripture. It is a branch that bears rich gospel fruit (Mt 8:17; 1 Pt 2:24; 1 Pt 2:4-6; Acts 8:32-33; Rv 5:6, 12; 13:8; 1 Pt 2:22; Rv 14:5; 1 Jn 3:5; Ro 5:19; Ro 4:25; Eph 5:2,25; Phil 2:7-9; Mk 15:28; Lk 22:37; Heb 9:28; Gal 4:27).

The tragedy of Old Testament kingdom seekers is that the vast majority of Abraham's descendents developed Tension Deficit Disorder. One group of religious libertines went the route of extreme permissiveness. "Do your own thing" became their model. Rather than living as God's pleasantly peculiar people, they lived as a perverse people. They imitated the pagan people around them. They even joined in the wretched practices of sacrificing their own children to sexual fertility cult gods.[67] Hedonism became their goal, their god, and their grave.[68]

Another group swung the opposite extreme into the orbit of extreme legalism. They piled human commandments upon commandments upon commandments obscuring the good news that salvation was God's gift. Rather than God's mercy and steadfast love being the centerpiece of theology, a salvation system that centered on human effort replaced a foundation of grace. The temple worship system deteriorated. By the time Jesus arrived on the scene, there were more than 9,000 priests connected with the temple in Jerusalem. Religious leaders in Jerusalem developed beyond the Torah and the prophets all manner of laws. These laws focused on the sacrifices of lambs and rams, and held those sacrifices above all others should be made in Jerusalem. This turned Zion into a crass commercial center rather than a place for Jews and Gentiles to come to learn about the anticipated Messiah who would bring rich spiritual blessings to the world.[69]

By God's grace, a remnant of believers remained. (Isaiah 1:9; Amos 3:12; 5:15) They were people who did not get swallowed up by the seductions of legalism and lawlessness. Moreover, while they did not know the radical lengths to which Yahweh would go—doing for the world what God had asked of Abraham at Moriah—they saw the paradoxical threads of the Hebrew Scriptures. They saw how the coming Messiah would be both a victorious king and a suffering servant. They lived in that tension expressed by John the Baptizer, "Behold the Lamb of God who would take away the sin of the world." (John 1:29)

Paradox in service of the gospel in the Old Testament was to remind people that the kingdom of God would come in a wholly different way than natural man could imagine. Many people within Israel fell into the trap of taking a fraction of the messianic formula, cutting out the theology of the cross that is latent in the first gospel promise, (Genesis 3:15) and loaded in Isaiah's suffering servant song. (Isaiah 53) Isaiah 53 is a detailed commentary on Genesis 3:15. Written in the past tense and speaking of the future—in profound paradoxical style—Isaiah describes elements of Good Friday as if he is standing at the foot of the cross. He makes clear that the ultimate battle Messiah would fight is a spiritual battle entailing cosmic implications. The world bruised Messiah's heels so the nations could heal. Mankind's sins crushed the Messiah so that he could crush the one who seduced our first parents into double extremes. After all, did not Adam and Eve immediately break into lawlessness and legalism after their uprising against God, blundering wildly and blaming profusely everyone but themselves?

Throughout the ages in Old Testament times, the masses would be so brutal to the prophets that it seemed as if the whole promise of a spiritual Savior was in doubt. (Amos 2:12) Nevertheless, God kept for himself an Elijah-like remnant. This nevertheless of God's faithfulness would, for the remnant, become the basis for the grand nevertheless of faith for the faithful. Habakkuk cries out how believing is seeing even though the cattle stalls are empty, the stock market kaput, and trials are at our doorsteps in spades. Nevertheless, because of the Savior God and the gift of salvation, Yahweh is worthy of our trust. (Habakkuk 3:17-19) Habakkuk's hymn of faith moved Luther to write these lines in his grand hymn of faith, *A Mighty Fortress Is Our God*: "Take they our life, goods, fame, wife and child. Let these all be gone, They yet have nothing won: The Kingdom ours remaineth!"

Chapter 7

New Testament Paradoxes

St. Augustine adroitly summarized the relationship of the paradoxical Old Testament with the paradoxical New Testament. He said, "The Old Testament is the New Testament revealed, and the New Testament is the Old Testament concealed."[70] Luther, a Hebrew scholar of the first rank, noticed the same nexus. Once, Luther quipped, "The Bible is the cradle and the Christ child is the baby in the cradle."[71] Without Jesus as linchpin, the Old Testament's theological strands of suffering servant and king end up detached, displaced, and dispersed. Tension Deficit Disorder arises. Extreme ideologues of the legalistic or lawless stripe oppress and depress the people.

Without Jesus as the hinge of history, the first gospel promise (Genesis 3:15) would become unhinged. Apart from Jesus, it makes no sense. Apart from Jesus, there is no one to overcome by way of a tree (the cross) the ones who were overcome by a tree in the garden. Through Jesus, who embodies the absolute paradox, we see how all of history, life, and eternity focuses upon trees: the tree in the garden, (Genesis 2:9) the tree of Golgotha, (John 19:17) and the tree of paradise. (Revelation 22:2) Three trees tell the story of life through the Lord of life who subjects himself to death in order to tie together the meaning of all of this.

Paradox as a concept rips through the New Testament in a profuse, profound, and plentiful manner.

Wherever Jesus went, his actions, axioms, and antidotes were high paradox. Luke, the physician, caught this pattern in his gospel. He tells a story about how Jesus healed a man paralyzed. However, the healing of this paralyzed man is not the greatest gift Jesus grants. He bestows upon the man forgiveness of sins, the gift that brings life and salvation. (Luke 5:25-26) Some of the Pharisees and religious teachers of the law could not live with this tension. They were furious with Jesus. Swallowing camels and straining gnats, the various defenders of legalism and lawlessness find no comfort that this poor soul was healed, absolved, and became whole.

These religious leaders ended up in the land of extremism and heartlessness because their concept of the Messiah suffered a severe theological deficit. Even though the Psalmist linked forgiveness and healing (Psalm 103:1-3) as something that came from Yahweh, that connection was simply not on the radar screen of these religious leaders. They were closed-minded to any possibility that the suffering servant healer of mankind (Isaiah 53) might be among them. As a whole, the people present that day were not blinded by TDD. They responded to what they saw and heard with a face value reaction. Luke records the reaction in this fashion: "And utter amazement seized all, and they glorified God and were filled with fear, saying, 'We have seen paradoxical things today.'"[72]

Dr. Arthur Just's apt translation of *paradoxical things* the people saw is no paraphrase. The people who witnessed the healing of the paralytic were confused that a man would do God-like things. Strange, seemingly contradictory, polar opposites were at work. Nevertheless, this was the way Yahweh worked, and it was the way Jesus, as Messiah, ushered in the kingdom of God.

Although this is the sole instance in the New Testament where the Greek word meaning *paradox* is used, paradox as a concept rips through the New Testament in a profuse, profound, and plentiful manner. The New Testament's use of paradox is not just to present the unusual and strange. Instead, the paradoxes convey vital, in-depth truths about the mystery of the kingdom of God. Consequently, it is of little surprise to see how Jesus dovetails the parabolic with the paradoxical.

With a number of parables of Jesus, one sees paradoxes that revealed "mysteries of the kingdom." (Matthew 13:11) In fact, one witnesses the prophet from Nazareth unveiling a double paradox in the parable known as the "Laborers in the Vineyard." (Matthew 20:1-16) When Jesus concludes this parable with the paradox, "So the last shall be first, and the first last," (Matthew 20:16) Jesus hearkens how God will create the new Israel much as he created the Israel of old. In grace, God will draw the lost, the last, and the least likely people to become members of this kingdom.

Paradoxes are a superb tool to reveal significant facts about the kingdom of God because God's kingdom is paradoxical to the core. In what sense is it paradoxical? The kingdom of God is paradoxical in its presence, the person who embodies it, its purpose, its pedagogy, its people, its parousia today and its parousia tomorrow.[73]

First, the kingdom of God is paradoxical in its presence among us in the here and now. In the gospel of Mark we hear how "Jesus came into Galilee preaching the gospel of the kingdom, and saying, 'The time is fulfilled, and the kingdom of God is at hand.' " (Mark 1:14) These striking words in Mark find support throughout the New Testament, a document that thoroughly affirms that God's kingdom of grace has, in a real sense, become present fact here and now. John Bright aptly describes how the kingdom of God is a rich reality, a power at work in the world:

> The future tense of the Old Testament ("behold the days are coming,") and the like has now become an emphatic present: "The kingdom

> of God is at hand." (Mark 1:15) The final act of the drama has even now begun, the messianic age has dawned; he who is greater than Solomon, greater than Jonah, (Luke 11:31-32) nay greater than the temple and law, (Matthew 12:6-8) is here. The Servant is even now on the scene, (Luke 4:17-21) and all may see his works. (Matthew 11:2-6) This is the day which all the past desired to see, but did not. (Luke 10:23-24) No need any more to look wildly for signs of the Kingdom's imminent coming: it is right here "among you." (Luke 17:21) In the person and work of Jesus, the kingdom of God has intruded into the world.[74]

The paradox of the kingdom of God's presence is part of what is known as the "yet, not yet" tension of the kingdom. Indeed, the kingdom is among us now in the person of Christ the Lord. Nevertheless, believers in Christ also pray that it will yet come, praying, "thy kingdom come." (Matthew 6:10) Here we see squarely the paradox; namely, that the kingdom is at one and the same time realized, yet unrealized. Similarly, when Christians pray, "thy will be done on earth, as it is in heaven," (Matthew 6:10) they pray paradoxically as people who are under God's gracious rule yet who have not entered into the full consummation of the kingdom. In the same way, the fifth petition is a prayer for the gift we already have, the forgiveness of sins. (Luke 11:4) A close inspection of the Lord's Prayer is a study in both paradox and the "yet, not yet" reality tension of the kingdom of God. Every petition echoes the paradoxical tension of the "yet, not yet" so we do not slip into the ditch of pride nor despair.

Second, the kingdom of God is paradoxical in the person who embodies it, Jesus Christ. Understanding of the paradoxical nature of Christ's person is essential because the kingdom of God comes among us (Mark 1:15) and dwells within us (Galatians 2:20) in the person of Jesus Christ. How beautifully the Athanasian Creed formulates this when it speaks about Jesus in this majestic manner: "Equal to the Father as touching his Godhead and inferior to the Father as touching his manhood." There is no ADD and TDD here in this Christological confession.

Part and parcel of the incarnation is the paradox of the virgin birth. Ordinarily, the story of a pregnant virgin would have been an oxymoron in ancient days. Yet, with God, nothing is impossible. The only thing God cannot do is to sin because that would be going against His essence. Thus, he will not create a rock too big to budge, nor renege on his promises.

The paradox of the incarnation itself—God the Son assuming flesh—as well as the paradoxes that result from it, stretches across the pages of the New Testament. How the infinite God became finite without denying himself is a profound mystery that moves about in a reasonable fashion. It would be strange to think that God would not reveal himself in a strange manner lest there be no need for faith. However, this is the pattern of the Bible from Genesis to Revelation. Thus, at the same time, there is a wonderful reasonableness to the rhyme and revelation of the Bible (Luke 24:25-27) as well as deep mystery when it comes to matters like the incarnation. (1Timothy 3:16a) Reason gets into trouble only when it goes into an extreme mode—sitting in judgment of God's revelation—because of TDD, or when it concludes that God is not omnipotent enough to deliver all of what he promises. When reason fails to operate from the greater to the lesser, it is blinded by unbelief and the desire to either control by legalism or create hell on earth by lawlessness.

As one examines the paradox of the incarnation, the eyes of faith see how the absolute paradox begets paradox. The eyes of faith behold how he who sustains and holds the whole universe together (Colossians 1:17) becomes a dependent baby lying in a manger. (Luke 2:7) The eyes of faith, moved by the God of the impossible, delight in confessing how the one "in whom are hid all the treasures of wisdom" (Colossians 2:3) grows in wisdom. (Luke 2:40) The Spirit that moves one to confess that Jesus is Lord, (1 Corinthians 12:3) ruler over all things, moves one to be open to the paradoxical patterns that finite unbelief cannot find

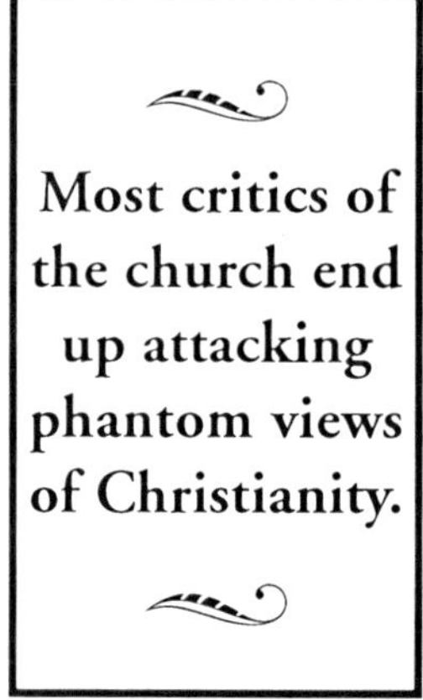

room for. Thus we marvel at how the bread of life (John 6:35) endures hunger, (Matthew 4:2) that the source of all waters (Hebrew 1:2) experiences thirst, (John 19:28) that the Son of God (Hebrews 4:15) learns obedience, (Hebrews 5:8) that the eternal God dies on a cross, (Luke 23:46) that the God who cannot die comes back to life, (Luke 24:6) that the one who saved others could not save himself, (Mark 15:31) that God forsakes God in hell, and God prays to God from hell. (Matthew 27:46)

The positive impact of the redemptive saving work of this paradoxical person is hard to begin to measure. English scholar Os Guinness suggests that eighty percent of the giving to charitable causes and hurting people throughout the world has had its roots in a culture influenced by Jesus and his compassion from the tree of paradox.[75] Rodney Stark, in his scholarly work, *The Victory of Reason*, shows how the person and work of Christ led to freedom, a capitalism tempered by the golden rule, and Western progress.

The irony here is that while human reason merits no credit in laying hold of faith in Christ, Christ lays hold of reason in a manner that gives birth to those things which are lovely, pure, true, just, commendable, excellent, and praiseworthy. (Philippians 4:9) In other words, the message of Christ upgrades reason. It provides for a coherent view of the universe through the Logos who created all things. (John 1:1, 3)

In light of the paradoxical death of Jesus as the world's greatest slave who brings cosmic freedom, (Philippians 2:5-11) Paul exhorts Christians, "Let your reasonableness be known to everyone." (Philippians 4:5) Where Christians get muddle-headed is when they harness fog from the fallen winds of the world. Specifically, when the breezes of legalism and lawlessness become part of the atmosphere of church bodies, reason goes berserk. It either sits in judgment of God's Word in irrational non sequitur ways or behaves in a suicidal fashion. In short, most critics of the church end up attacking phantom views of Christianity rather than a paradoxical gospel-centered view of Christianity. When historic Christianity is, at the same time, evolutionary and non-evolutionary, materialistic and non-materialistic, pro good works and not pro good works, inclusive as well as exclusive, then critics will find a challenging target to identify let alone dismantle.

If the Christian faith rests upon the Infinite who became finite without ceasing to be infinite, (Colossians 2:9) one should expect elements about this faith unlike any other faith, creed, or religion. No religion remotely comes close to presenting the paradoxes of Christianity or bringing to the world the blessings of historic Biblical Christianity. Dr. Philip Schaff once tried to capture the impact of the absolute paradox, Jesus Christ. Note the carefully crafted words of this nineteenth-century historian:

> Without money and arms He conquered more millions than Alexander, Caesar, Mohammed and Napoleon; without science and learning, He shed more light on things human and divine than all the philosophers and scholars combined; without the eloquence of the school, He spoke words of life such as were never spoken before, nor since, and produced effects which lie beyond the reach of orator or poet. Without writing a single line, He has set more pens in motion and furnished themes for more sermons, orations, discussions, works of art, learned volumes and sweet songs of praise than the whole army of great men of ancient and modern times. Born in a manger and crucified as a malefactor, He now controls the destinies of the civilized world and rules a spiritual empire which embraces one third of the inhabitants of the globe.[76]

When dealing with paradoxes, one observes how God gives paradoxes to answer paradoxical questions. For example, Job once asked, "How can one be clean that is born of a woman?" (Job 25:4) In other words, "how can God bring a clean thing from an unclean thing?" Through the miracle of the incarnation, by way of the prophesied virgin birth, through the work of the Holy Spirit (Luke 1:35) we see the paradoxical answer to this paradoxical question!

The gospel, with its many good news facets, is replete with paradoxes precisely because the embodiment of the gospel, Jesus Christ, lived a life brimming with paradoxes from his incarnation to his death and resurrection. Even now, as risen Savior, the paradox of his person remains as true God and true man. The post-ascension word reads, "For in him (Jesus) dwelleth all the fullness of the Godhead bodily." (Colossians 2:9) Even now, although Jesus suffers no more atonement pain, he still intimately identifies with the pain of his redeemed. (Acts 9:4; Matthew 25:40) At the same time, Jesus is transcendent and immanent!

Third, the purpose of Christ's coming into the world is paradoxical from beginning to end. He came into the world to defeat death by death. (Hebrews 2:14) He came into the world so the blind might see and those who see may turn blind. (John 9:39) He came into the world to give people a yoke so that their burdens might be light (Matthew 11:28-30) and a cross so that their joy might be full. (I John 1:4; 1 Corinthians 1:18) He, the sinless one, comes into the world to take upon Himself our sin so that we, the sinful ones, might receive his sinlessness. (2 Corinthians 5:21) At the heart of this happy exchange are deep mystery, diligent logical fulfilling of Old Testament prophecies, and daring paradox. (Isaiah 53)

When the apostle Paul wrote his first letter to the Corinthians asserting that the message of a crucified Messiah was an obstacle to the Jews and foolishness to the Greeks, (1 Corinthians 1:23) he also summarized the reaction of unbelief in the face of divine paradoxes. For Jews who grew up learning that cursed is he who died on a tree, (Deuteronomy 21:23) the message of the cross was especially jarring. That the core paradoxical idea embedded in the gospel entailed a Messiah becoming a curse to take away the curse of sin (Isaiah 53) was a scandal of highest proportion. Yet, God would use a scandal of one tree to take away the scandal caused by the first tree in the garden.

For Greeks, whose gods were often capricious, the sober yet staggering idea that the Creator would die for the creature was an unbearable feature. Yet, this is a crucial and unique truth of Christianity. In all other religions of the world, their gods really do not give a damn about the plight, peril, and problems of mankind. However, in Christianity we see that God does give a damn because he, himself, is willing to be damned for mankind's sin. For ancient Greeks as well as modern men and women, this too is a scandal because it spells out painfully what a serious matter is sin. If this is what it takes to forgive sins, that God through Jesus Christ must be a Yom Kippur sacrifice for the sins of the world, then here is huge humble pie. However, to those who believe this good news, this is God's power, God's wisdom, and God's paradoxically passionate way to save a fallen human race. (1 Corinthians 1:24)

Fourth, the pedagogical nature of the kingdom of God enlists paradox as a schoolmaster when it comes to style as well as substance. For example, when Jesus talks about religious leaders of his day straining gnats and swallowing camels, (Matthew 23:24) taking specks of dust out of the eyes of others while ignoring the big planks in their own eyes, (Matthew 7:4) mourning when they should have been rejoicing, and rejoicing when they should have been mourning, (Matthew 11:17) he is using paradoxical word pictures. It is part of his surgery of the soul, to put people to death through clean law so that he might cleanse and raise them through the gospel. (1 Corinthians 15:1-3) Moreover, his methodology is instructive, using paradoxical pictures in life to inculcate kingdom paradoxes.

The kingdom truths that come from the lips of our Lord are themselves permeated with paradoxes. One of his best-known paradoxes is, "He that findeth his life shall lose it; and he that loseth his life for my sake shall find it." (Matthew 10:39) Through this paradox, Jesus seeks to pave the way for the scandal of the cross as well as to reveal one of the secrets of joy. It is a way of saying that the key to happiness is to forget about happiness. When happiness becomes our main goal in life, it becomes our god. Heaven's happiness—joy—is a fruit of faith, not the root of faith. Joy rests in Jesus, the absolute paradox. Jesus tells us to seek first the gift of his kingdom and the gift of his righteousness, and all other needs would be satisfied. (Matthew 6:33)[77]

As I have sought to demonstrate, paradoxes often arise from a tension between texts. A good example is two seemingly contradictory teachings of our Lord from the very same gospel. In Matthew's gospel, Jesus says, "Blessed are the peacemakers." (Matthew 5:9) Yet, five chapters later, Jesus declares that he did not come to earth to bring peace, but a sword. (Matthew 10:34) What gives?

Years ago I preached a sermon on Matthew 10:34 proclaiming how Jesus was the Great Divide in history, beyond even A.D. and B.C. A visitor on that Lord's Day was quite upset with the sermon. This guest said my sermon was dark, disturbing, and troubling. This saint's evaluation caused me to do a double check on my sermon. While I could identify no false teaching per se, the sermon did suffer Tension Deficit Disorder. Upon reflection and repentance, I realized I could have done a better job holding together two ferocious tensions, namely, that Jesus is, at the same time, the Great Divide as well as the Great Reconciler in history. Where grace through faith embraces the gospel, royal reconciliation results from God's prior reconciliation of the world unto himself. (2 Corinthians 5:19-21) Divisions only deepen when the world rejects God's greatest gift.

In the July 1999 issue of the *Concordia Journal*, Dr. James Voelz, a New Testament scholar, wrote about these kinds of tensions in a most helpful article titled, *Newton and Einstein at the Foot of the Cross*.[78] To simplify this erudite article let me cut to the chase. Professor Voelz points out there are passages in the Bible that take on a Newton-like nature of perceiving reality while others take on an Einsteinian disposition. The Newton-like passages describe with accuracy the phenomenon that is taking place. The Einstein-like passages describe what is taking place behind the phenomenon. For example, you have a Newtonian text describing a phenomenon such as, "choose you this day whom ye will serve … but as for me and my house, we will serve the Lord." (Joshua

24:15) Contrast Joshua's words with this Einsteinian passage from the words of Jesus: "You have not chosen me, but I have chosen you, and ordained you, that ye should go and bring forth fruit." (John 15:16)

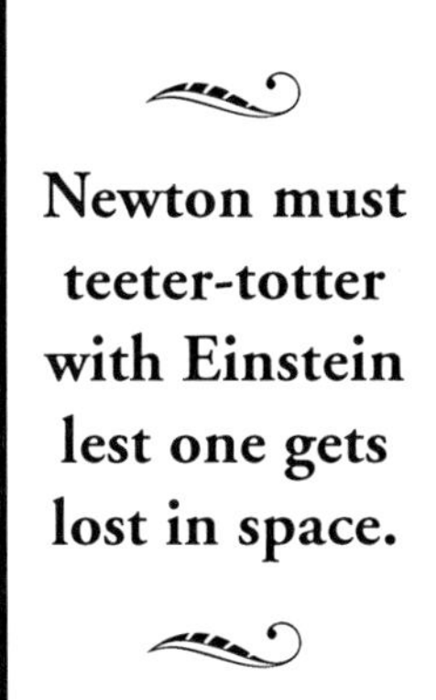
Newton must teeter-totter with Einstein lest one gets lost in space.

Which passage is right? Do we choose the Newtonian passage that puts the emphasis on people to make a decision? Or do we select the Einsteinian passage that explains what goes on behind the scene? God moves us to make the salutary choice. Both are correct. Yet, you must hold together the tension. Go too far with Newtonian hermeneutics and you end up in the extreme of legalism. Go too far with an Einstein-like approach and you will end up with the extreme of lawlessness. Newton must teeter-totter with Einstein lest one gets lost in space, overlooks grace, and gives man the place of God.

The radical nature of the gospel is that it challenges us to live in tension, be at ease with awkwardness, and give room for faith so that we can truly be human. St. Paul, a primetime paradoxicalist, knew the Greek world, grew up in the Hebrew world, and lived in the Roman world. Consequently, he could see things from multiple perches. By God's grace, this rich background caused him to revel in these kinds of tensions. Observe how he spliced Newton and Einstein together in his letter to the church at Philippi, "work out your salvation with fear and trembling [Newton], for it is God which worketh in you both to will and to act according to his good purpose" [Einstein].(Philippians 2:12b, 13) This passage contains a beautiful balance! There is no room for swallowing camels (lawlessness) or straining gnats (legalism)!

Earlier, I referred to the outstanding Baptist exegete A.T. Robertson. Keenly, he observed in his study how St. Paul sometimes sounds like Jacob Arminius, a Newton-like theologian, and other times sounds like John Calvin, who is more Einstein-like. Lutheran theology holds in tension elements of theology that Arminius and Calvin each stretched too far at the expense of their own theological counterweights. Both were fine Christian men who had a deep love for the Savior and the Bible. Each sought to emphasize a particular facet of the gospel. Where do we find common ground with them and where do we lovingly disagree?

With the brilliant Calvin, we agree that God, in love and through Christ, chooses who will go to heaven. These choices God made even before he laid the foundation of the universe. The triune God loved us before we existed. God, the Father, serves as the administrator of this salvation. Jesus, the Son, serves as the agent. The Holy Spirit administrates it. All of this St. Paul beautifully weaves into one long sentence in the Greek. (Ephesians 1:3-14) Paul does this to hold in tension some heavy-duty doctrine to keep us from the remotest realm of legalism. Later, he will provide counterbalances to ward off lawlessness.

Yet, we disagree with Calvin who stated that God also chose who would go to hell. Nowhere in Scripture do we see this taught. It is a deduction without foundation. Nor do we see Scripture teaching that Jesus did not die for all people, a teaching that this Reformer (Calvin) advanced. On the contrary, the Bible teaches that Jesus "died for all." (2 Corinthians 5:15, 19) This truth of the gospel is so important! Why? Because if Jesus died for all, we know he died for each one of us as individuals. Jesus is, as John the Baptist proclaimed, "The Lamb of God who takes away the sin of the world." (John 1:29) While we salute so much of what Calvin has taught, here I believe that this giant of the faith suffered a theological form of Tension Deficit Disorder.

In a similar fashion, I believe that Jacob Arminius went too far in the opposite direction. Arminius rejected the doctrine of election by grace. Little did he realize the implication of this rejection. By rejecting the doctrine of election, Arminius threw overboard the notion of salvation by grace alone (Ephesians 2:8,9) and stumbled headlong into the ditch of legalism. Also, and I believe unwittingly, he brought into his worldview the very dangerous idea that humans can do something apart from God, the Almighty. Arminius believed we could make choices on our own, thus rendering God to be merely semi-almighty. In the case of John

Calvin, he was rejecting universal grace just as Jacob Arminius ended up rejecting salvation by grace alone. In each instance, the issue is one of grace, gospel, and God's goodness.

Lutheran theology seeks to take the golden middle in these matters. We do it so that the doctrine of grace does not suffer. Whereas Arminius and most Protestant Christians teach zero predestination, and whereas Calvinist Christians teach double predestination, Lutherans teach single predestination. If we Lutherans are right on this matter, does it make us any better than any other Christians? I say absolutely and positively not! The advantage of our position is simply this: It gives all glory to God for the gift of salvation (Amen, brother Calvin!) and allows us to comfort people with the truth that Jesus died for all. (Amen, brother Arminius!) In short, we get to keep the best of brother John and brother Jacob! This is a theological win/win position rooted in Scripture, grounded in grace, and doubled in its comforting!

Only by taking a paradoxical position like this on the weighty matter of predestination can one keep from developing a truncated gospel. Wrote Adolf Köberle, "St. Paul (1 Corinthians 9:27) and Luther have understood much more profoundly this paradox of God's sole activity in working salvation and of human responsibility for its loss, which is incomprehensible to reason."[79] On an Einstein-like level, the doctrine of grace alone election does make sense while on the Newton-like level it eludes us. Why some are saved and not others is a mystery that the Christian church has thought best to adore rather than to over-explore. If a person ends up in heaven, God's grace accomplishes it: if they end up in hell, the culpability belongs to mankind. Remember, there must be some room for faith!

Whether Einstein and Newton, or Mary and Martha, God's initiative at work or human concurrence, the Bible is beautifully balanced. Such balance seeks to hold high Christ as Savior as well as the one who is most worthy to imitate. (Ephesians 5:1-2) Such balance keeps one out of the bed of legalism as well as out of the brothel of lawlessness. Such Biblical balance and paradoxical pathways give striving minds the impulse to distinguish, yet to hold together, these ferocious opposites. Indeed, the pedagogical paradoxes are teaching tools used by the Holy Spirit in service of the gospel.

One of the highly instructive and highly comforting paradoxes in the New Testament is a resurrection paradox in which Jesus, as the resurrection and the life, declares that "he that believeth in me, though he were dead, yet shall he live: And whosoever liveth and believeth in me shall never die." (John 11:24-25) Other comforting paradoxes that the Spirit gives us for our education and edification, as well as for our perspective and perseverance, are: "when I am weak, I am strong;" (2 Corinthians 12:10) "whom the Lord loves he chastens;" (Hebrews 12:6) "blessed are the poor in spirit;" (Matthew 5:3) "blessed are those who mourn;" (Matthew 5:4) and "the meek shall inherit the earth." (Matthew 5:5)[80]

The last three verses from the Beatitudes form the opening part of Jesus' Sermon on the Mount. Each shines with paradoxical imprint. Those who are poor in spirit are open to be rich in God. The followers of Jesus are joyful mourners who mourn over their sins and rejoice over the forgiveness of those sins. They hold in tension Matthew 5:4 with Philippians 4:4, "Rejoice in the Lord always!" The meek are the gentle-strong who find strength in Christ's weakness upon the cross, a weakness that overcomes the strongest foes and forces found in the universe.

Throughout the Sermon on the Mount, paradoxes rooted in the wisdom of ages enlighten us. Thomas Jefferson thought so highly of the Sermon of the Mount as the highest formulation of ethics that he used tax money to produce and propagate this sermon so that America might have a more enlightened citizenry. Part of the attraction for Jefferson regarding the Sermon on the Mount was the balance that Jesus demonstrated in his teaching. It was this kind of balance that would need to be present in the thinking of the leaders of a young nation as they formed a government of checks and balances.

Fifth, the kingdom of God is paradoxical in the people who are part of it. On the one hand, we call the people of the kingdom of God saints. This is not something they merit, but rather they inherit this status through the gift of faith and forgiveness that God grants for the sake of Jesus. Ephesians alone refers nine times to the redeemed as saints. (1:1; 1:15; 1:18; 2:19; 3:8; 3:18; 4:12; 5:3; 6:18) On the other hand and at the same time, God's people remain sinners. (1 John 1:7-10) The paradox that we are at the same time sinner and saint is intended to both warn and to comfort us. It warns us against any omnipotence (John 15:5c) while at the same time it assures us that we are part of a holy nation. (1 Peter 2:9) Such a view accounts for a present reality of sin even after faith in Christ, as well as the reality of Christ's righteousness being ours through faith. In short, it is another expression of the "yet, not yet" nature of the kingdom.

It is easy for Christians—even well educated clergy!—to swing wildly one way or the other regarding this paradox. Years ago, I was attending a St. Louis pastor's conference where this paradox was unwittingly being dissected by TDD clergy. One segment of the gathered pastors was bemoaning the emphasis in Sunday morning worship that accented "we are poor miserable sinners" and "worms." (Romans 7:24; Isaiah 41:14) They said joy is the name of the game when it comes to worship. The other group of pastors vigorously argued that we must emphasize the dark side of life even after conversion. Back and forth, these two sides played the game of theological ping-pong. After a good spell of listening, Dr. Armin Moellering got up and said, "Brothers, I am here to tell you that I am a poor miserable sinner and a worm, but I am a joyful poor miserable sinner and a happy worm!" Game. Set. Match.

Dr. Moellering caught wisely in his down-to-earth way this sinner/saint tension. Good Greek scholar that he was, Dr. Moellering realized, despite this "poor miserable sinner status" that yet remains this side of heaven, the Bible also teaches that we are now glorified. (Romans 8:30) The use of the aorist tense of the word *glorified* stresses that our glorification is a done deal! To be sure, the full fruits of this

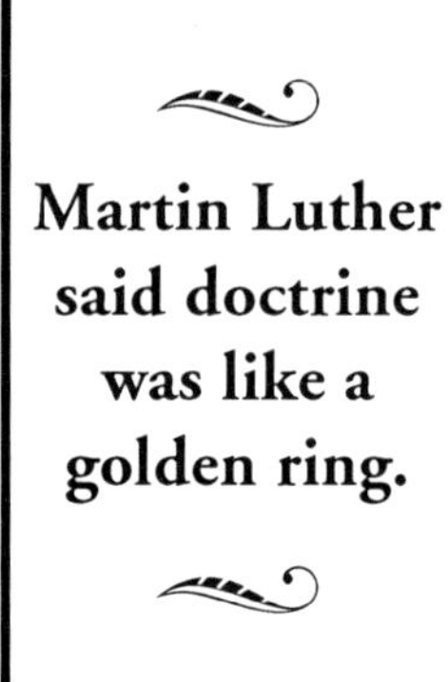

glorification await us; (1 Corinthians 15:43) nevertheless, we are simultaneously glorified; yet not glorified.

As paradoxical people—a peculiar people, pilgrim people—God's people move through this life to the beat of a different drum than people who live life "under the sun." (Ecclesiastes 1:14) The apostle Paul describes the paradoxical pattern of our earthly sojourn in a way that is part descriptive and part prescriptive: "As unknown yet well known; as dying, and behold, we live; as chastened and not killed; As sorrowful, yet always rejoicing; as poor, yet making many rich; as having nothing, and yet possessing all things (2 Corinthians 6:9, 10).[81] This is the life of the "yet, not yet" people of God.

Scores of other paradoxes shape the actions and thinking of God's people. It is part of the pattern where God afflicts the comfortable and comforts the afflicted. For example, it is to the elect that St. Paul says, "Wherefore let him that thinketh he standeth take heed lest he fall." (1 Corinthians 10:13) The elect fall? Never! Nonetheless, we must warn the elect. What a glorious tension! It slays legalism and lawlessness, the swallowing of camels and the straining of gnats, all in one swoop.

Martin Luther said doctrine was like a golden ring. It is all connected. It all hangs together. In addition, if doctrine indeed is a golden ring, then paradox must be the rim of the ring, providing Spirit-designed parameters to keep us from exaggerating one truth at the expense of another. Such a golden ring with such a royal rim keeps one from accepting wedding ring proposals from Lady Legalism and Lady Lawlessness, from Princess "I have to be in control" and Princess "I want to do whatever the hell I want." Each is a tyrant with simply a different modus operandi.

Sixth, the kingdom of God is paradoxical in the nature of its *parousia* today. The danger of scores of books that treat the subject of Christ's second coming (*parousia*) is that they say less than little about the nature of his coming today. Yet, this is crucial for a person to grow in the grace and knowledge of our Lord and Savior Jesus Christ. (2 Peter 2:18)

Just as Jesus entered time and space by way of the incarnation, he comes to us paradoxically today. Through simple acts, Jesus grants grace. Through the apostolic acts of baptism, the Lord's Supper, holy absolution, and the preaching of the gospel, God's paradoxical people participate in his coming to us today. Through these acts of love, God grants us spiritual strength, grace, and mercy.

So, what is the paradox here? Adolf Köberle identifies the nature of this paradox in a superb manner. He writes: "The paradox of Lutheranism, 'the more external—the more internal' [*extra nos—in nobis*] is always incomprehensible to natural thinking or party feeling."[82] Through these sure signs, through these means of grace markers, through these vessels of love, God comes in the form of the Holy Spirit. He does it this way so that spiritual baloney salesmen or philosophical hot air experts do not take us in. He does this so that neither rabid rationalism nor murky mysticism kills or clouds our faith in Christ. He does this to continue the pattern of his incarnation, coming to us in humble strange ways, his ways. Through his ways and means, these gospel dispensing modes, Jesus paradoxically forgives our sins, gives us everlasting life, and grants us eternal salvation. It is a Jesus thing so we pay close attention to it.

Consider the gospel's paradoxical nature of baptism as a case in point. Baptism is a drowning that saves. (1 Peter 3:20-21) Flat out, the Bible says that Jesus saves through baptism. From another angle, St. Paul spells out this truth in Romans. He speaks of baptism as the life-giving death whereby we "were baptized into Jesus Christ into his death ...buried with him by baptism into death: that just as Christ was raised up from the dead by the glory of the Father, even so we also should walk in newness of life." (Romans 6:3b, 4) Paul enunciates the implications of this real baptism into the very death of Christ as a life-giving event. He does so when he reveals, "For by one Spirit are we all baptized into one (risen) body." (1 Corinthians 12:13) The apostle wants Christians to know that throughout life, even until death, even until the last day, this "washing of regeneration and renewing of the Holy Ghost" (Titus 3:5) is in force to help us participate in the daily life-giving death of repentance.

Similarly, the Lord's Supper manifests a real paradoxical character with deep gospel dimensions. Its paradoxical and *parousia*-like nature consists in the fact that in this holy meal bread and wine are not merely offered but also—at the same time—become the body and blood of the Risen Savior who fills the whole universe according to his and human nature. (Colossians 2:9) Notice the path of the golden middle here once again. While one group of Christians believes the bread and wine disappear, and while another group of Christians believes that this meal only represents Christ's body and blood, paradox threads a needle. With utmost earnestness, it embraces the paradox put forth by St. Paul, "The cup of blessing which we bless, is it not the communion of the blood of Christ? The bread which we break, is it not the communion of the body of Christ?" (1 Corinthians 10:16)

When we do not overlook the profound paradoxical nature of the Lord's Supper, we see a double cosmic connection. We see a breathtaking connection between the *parousia* of Christ's coming in the Lord's Supper among us now and his *parousia* at the end of time. However, when we reduce this meal to no more than a sacred pantomime, we miss gargantuan gospel, colossal comfort, added assurance, and precious pardoning strength. The Lord's Supper is much more than a spiritual exercise to remember that Jesus died for us. It is a major mystery of imparting to us the medicine of immortality. Herman Sasse explains this double *parousia* connection:

> Much rather the hope of the Lord's return and the coming Kingdom is so powerfully alive in this celebration because the Lord's Supper, as the celebration of Christ's real presence, already includes a fulfillment of that expectation. Whoever partakes of it already now sits at the table of the Lord, whose guest he will be one day in the kingdom of God. The same Lord, whose coming in glory one implores in the Eucharistic prayer is already present in the celebration of the Eucharist.

> Thus the prayer "Come, Lord Jesus" retains its eschatological meaning, but at the same time it carries the meaning expressed in early liturgical prayer… "Be present, be present, Jesus good priest, among us, as also you will be in the midst of your disciples."[83]

The paradoxical, *parousia*-nature of holy absolution, another means of grace, deserves attention as well. Again, this is another way that Jesus comes to us in time and in space, granting us his favor and his forgiveness. So important is this gift that it was one of the very first things Jesus did after he rose bodily from the dead. (John 20:19-23) Unfortunately, Christians often gloss over this stupendous gift, spiritualizing it as a result of ADD and TDD.

The paradoxical nature of this means of grace by which Christ imparts forgiveness, (John 20:23) bestows upon us his Holy Spirit, (John 20:22) and grants peace, (John 20:21) is not unlike an aspect of the virgin birth of our Lord. Like the virgin birth, God brings forth a clean thing from an unclean thing in holy absolution. He uses sinful people to forgive sins and to be a means by which the Holy Spirit comes. He gives dying people the most awesome authority and life-giving message in the universe! For in holy absolution there is every bit as much power at work as when God said, "Let there be light!" That dying, sinful people should impart by mouth a life-giving sinlessness, under the authority of Christ, is certainly a paradoxical movement.[84]

Holy absolution is not only a way in which God again brings a clean thing from an unclean thing, but it keeps Christians centered. It reminds us that the entire life of the Christian is one of repentance fueled by the forgiveness and love of Jesus. Such a life that drinks from Christ's love and constant forgiveness has less and less desire to swallow camels (lawlessness) and strain gnats (legalism).

This paradoxical path and *parousia*-nature of the preaching and teaching of the gospel itself, as well as the paradoxical nature of God's people, is a huge theme of Scripture. Through the cornerstone of Christ, by the touchstones of Word and Sacrament, the Spirit produces living

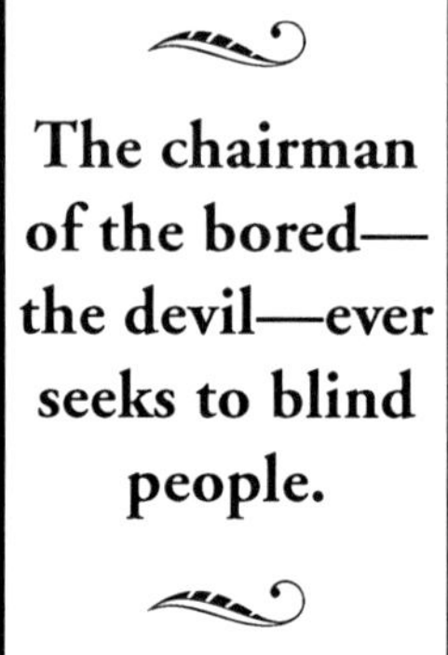

stones, (1 Peter 2:5) yet another paradox! Martin Luther summarizes eloquently the paradoxical and *parousia* work of the Spirit when he declares how the Holy Spirit "calls, gathers, enlightens, and sanctifies the whole Christian church on earth and keeps it with Jesus Christ in the one true faith."[85]

A paradoxical view of reality under the gospel alerts one to the dangers of Tension Deficit Disorder. At the same time, this equips one to see how easy it is to swallow camels and strain gnats. At the same time, a paradoxical view of reality stirs the soul and fires the imagination to think of the living God in ways that far surpass the boring, false, one-dimensional images peddled by all salvation-by-works religions. The chairman of the bored—the devil—ever seeks to blind people by seducing them to run with one truth at the expense of the opposite and balancing truth.

The 9/11 Commission, in the summer of 2004, issued a meticulously detailed report indicating reasons for the U.S. government's failure to avert the terrorist attacks of September 11, 2001. At the top of the commission's list was "lack of imagination." The report indicated, "Imagination is not a gift usually associated with bureaucracies." How true. For church bodies to be effective in the coming century, they must know how the coming Christ comes to us in time, space, and the greatness of his person and work. Through the means of grace of word and sacrament, the Holy Spirit comes to us in ways far beyond our imagination to help us avert boredom and avoid extremes.[86] The only alternative is to end up gulping camels and grabbing gnats.

At the same time, we must ever see the danger of the two lethal L's: lawlessness gorges itself on camels while legalism specializes at gnat-o-technology. Both are blind. A theology that centers on the majesty of Jesus and how he comes to us according to his arrangements, only that theology—covered with love—will enlighten. It will help us be faithful and flexible, humble and bold, avoiding gospel reductionism (swallowing camels) and gospel restrictionism (gnat straining). The paradoxical God of reality, the God of Abraham, Isaac, and Jacob, the Three-in-One God of all grace, enables us to do far more than we dare to imagine. (Ephesians 3:20)

About two weeks before the 9/11 attacks upon our nation by fanatical specialists who excelled in swallowing camels (lawless) and straining gnats (legalists), I spoke with one of the highest-ranking government officials on National Security and Intelligence. I asked him if the hot geo-political issue of the world was Israel and the Palestinian matter. He said, "Pastor Pete, we are always very concerned about that region of the world. That is not our major concern now. To tell you the truth, we are scared to death about a terrorist attack, but we don't know how or when it will happen."

Lack of imagination, a fruit of Tension Deficit Disorder, blinds one from seeing a wider picture of reality. The terrorists were so holier-than-thou in their insecure feelings of superiority; they launched an utterly lawless attack upon people that had done them no harm. Had they known of the deep paradoxical love of Jesus for all people and the meaning of Jesus' death, they would never have set out upon such a diabolical path as the one they did. Soberly, it would not be the worst thing in the world to remind terrorists that there are degrees of hell. Jesus taught this to knock people off their high horse of holier-than-thou-ism as well as a means to assuage a measure of murder and mayhem.

Throughout our nation's history, we have had our own kind of Tension Deficit Disorder. We minimize the evil that fanatics can do. We get complacent. We do not realize the more people strain gnats, the bigger is the chance that they will swallow a camel.

Step back in history to December 7, 1941. Our government had excellent intelligence that an attack was coming from Japan. The problem? Our government could not imagine the attackers would set aim at Hawaii. Our experts were only focusing on the Southeast Asia realm. They suffered Tension Deficit Disorder by fixing on only one line of thinking.

Not long ago I read a book in preparation for a youth leadership seminar titled, "Why Smart Executives Fail." As the author, Sydney Finkelstein, described the meltdown of a number of corporations and their executives, a pattern emerged: the lack of a paradoxical mindset. Leadership requires a balancing act of vision and details, big picture and small picture implemented in a simultaneous fashion. Finkelstein's conclusion reminded me of a saying, "All the good stuff in the end is in the Bible."

A hobby of mine is the study of the paradoxical mindset of the founders and framers of our nation. Without a paradoxical mindset there would have been no way the birth of a democratic Republic would ever have occurred. In addition, there would have been no paradoxical mindset to fight the extremes had the key figures of the early history of our nation not been steeped in the Bible. Granted, some of the key architects were not what we would call evangelical Christians. Neither were most of them deists; actually only about five percent, at best, were true deists, and that estimate is being generous. The vast majority had Christian roots and Judeo-Christian sensibilities when it came to the law of God as the necessary gun and glue for this Republic.

Regarding the paradoxical mindset of the framers and founders, you see it in James Madison who recognized the long roots of original sin. Thus, he writes paradoxically in *The Federalist Papers, Number 51,* that there is a need to "let ambition counteract ambition." The last classes Madison took before graduating from Princeton were in Hebrew studies. He took them under the conservative Calvinist worldview of Princeton's brilliant president James Witherspoon, a man who taught and influenced a host of key men present at the forming of our nation. To its credit, the Calvinist worldview had a very good understanding of human nature that was crucial to the whole concept of separation of powers. A good Calvinist as well as a good Lutheran can easily resonate to the observation that "anyone who believes in total depravity can't be all bad." At the same time, we give room for that little voice box in our mind called the conscience to signal right and wrong. This is yet another high wire tension Scripture presents that echoes reality and history.

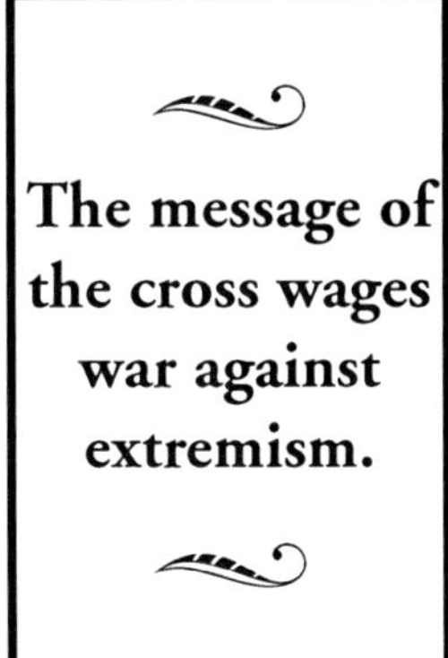

Earlier we saw how, when it came to matters of church and state, James Madison, George Washington, Benjamin Franklin and others viewed matters dialectically. They, along with Alexander Hamilton, John Adams, Thomas Jefferson, and John Jay, believed that the relationship of church and state should be one of functional interaction and institutional separation—a paradox! They wanted to avoid two extremes: One, a church state. Two, the complete separation of church and state. The French Revolution subscribed to the latter and staggered into a bloody reign of terror, heads chopped off, loss of due process of the law, and anarchy that morphed into totalitarianism under the boot of Napoleon.[87]

The point of this excursus is to show how the influence of Christianity and its paradoxical worldview positively influences culture wherever the gospel goes. For when this message takes root, the message of the cross wages war against extremism. Ironically, God had to take extreme measures to put into time and space a message and means that not only create faith and love, but also turn hearts toward a life that reclaims a measure of balance this side of heaven. Just as the cross took a terrorist under misguided authority by the name of Saul and turned him into a man of peace, the story of Good Friday and Easter remains the only hope for mankind. It is the only message that simultaneously slays anarchy and totalitarianism, sectarianism and syncretism, lawlessness and legalism, swallowing camels and straining gnats. Only the wounds of God hanging on a cross can heal this wounded world.

Chapter 8

A Paradoxical Vision of the End Times

Martin Luther said that we should read history like the Hebrew Bible—backwards. Time management experts tell us that when we plan anything we should always have a view of the end in mind. In order to read the times, at the same time we must view them in light of the eternities. Only then will our vision of life be truly relevant as well as timeless.

I believe vision necessary for maximum insight needs to be rooted in the end-time facets of the paradoxical gospel. Apart from an end-times vision through the person and work of the absolute paradox, one is bound to feel like one is living in a cosmic squirrel cage devoid of rhyme, reason, and hope. Without a paradoxical vision of the end times, one is likely to conclude that history is no more than, "a tale told by an idiot, full of sound and fury, signifying nothing."[88]

In New Testament nomenclature the end times encompasses the whole New Testament age beginning with the incarnation of our Lord, stretching to his second coming. The *eschaton* (last days), according to Hebrews 1:2, were inaugurated when the Word became flesh, "but in these last days God has spoken to us by His Son." On Pentecost Day, the apostle Peter proclaimed that the *eschaton* (last days) had arrived.

Citing the prophet Joel, Peter declared that the last days were upon them: "No, this is what was spoken by the prophet Joel: 'In the last days, God says, I will pour out my Spirit on all people.'" (Acts 2:16, 17) About this passage, F.F. Bruce asserts, "The 'last days' began with Christ's first advent and will end with his second advent; they are days which the age to come overlaps the present age."[89]

Special attention to a paradoxical vision of the end times is crucial for Christians who live in the 21st century. Without a paradoxical vision, the weight of the difficult days before us will be crushing. We witness this escalating despair coming from many intellectual quarters. For example, in 2003, Martin Rees, a highly respected Cambridge astronomer, made a sobering prediction: the odds of human survival by the end of this century are no more than fifty-fifty.[90] The good news from his point of view: science is advancing at an awesome rate. The bad news from his perch: there is a dark side to this exhilarating explosion of knowledge. Catastrophes could come from mad scientists, anarchists, religious extremists, nuclear explosions, geneticists, or worldwide epidemics—wherever wisdom and moderation do not temper knowledge.

Stanley Rothman, a think tank researcher for Forbes, has studied the cultural landscape of the Western world for decades. Rothman, an agnostic sociologist/political scientist, arrived a decade ago at gloomy conclusions for our declining society. With a keen outsider's analysis, he revealed the Tension Deficit Disorder that plagues today's Protestant tradition. Peter Brimelow, a writer for Forbes, summarizes Rothman's assessment of contemporary culture:

> This religious (Protestant Christianity) may be self-destructing. Its very rationality is undercutting the religious basis for its values. And its very economic success has financed the rise of what Rothman calls 'cultural strategic elites'—influential groups like his major media professionals and academics—who are divorced from the system and, his polls show, increasingly hostile to it.[91]

A well-respected voice within Lutheran circles reverberates similar concerns as Rothman. Dr. Robert Kolb, from Concordia Seminary in St. Louis, Mo., detects a crumbling civility in culture, gravitation toward the ditch of dissolution. He has written,

> "Although we do not like to hear it, it is possible that North American society has gone too far to be salvaged; its exploitation of the poor and needy may cry to heaven for such a judgment as we cannot imagine."[92]

While Sir Martin Rees and Stanley Rothman view reality with a keen eye, they do not have the enhanced vision the cosmic Christ grants through faith. They do not have faith toward the future based on what God has done in the past—hope. Through faith, one sees a clear picture of the increasing birth-pang problems of this world in light of the predictions of Jesus. (Matthew 24:7-8) As Martin Franzmann put it, "All history alerts the disciple for the end of history."[93] Furthermore, we know that history will not end a single second before the Lord of history, Jesus Christ, determines it is time for the curtain to come down. (Matthew 25:31-46) Until that time, the disciple is to be composed and ready. We are to keep our vessels of oil filled by vigorously appropriating God's grace through word and sacrament, fellowship and prayer. (Matthew 25:1-13) Through this engagement, the wicks of faith burn brightly in this dark world.

Such a flame of faith will help us live as Luther encourages; live as though Christ died yesterday, rose today, and is coming tomorrow. Faith in the Savior who has come, is coming, and will yet come enables the child of God to avoid Attention Deficit Disorder regarding the end times. It helps us avoid despair over the dissolution of all things, moves us to work for the betterment of things, and keeps extremes from devouring us. In an odd way, the worse things get, the more Christian hope should rise. (Luke 21:28)

Above all, faith will help us see how Jesus is the head of history, the hinge of history, and the hope of history. This paradoxical vision will allow us to see how Jesus, in the midst of all things, is ever working everything together for the good of his bride, the church. (Ephesians 1:20-23) At the same time, it will energize us to abound in the work of the Lord, (1 Corinthians 15:58) especially leading people to Jesus through the gospel; for once a person comes to faith in Christ, he or she always wants to bring someone along to heaven.

Because the field of what theologians call eschatology (end times) has such a breadth, length, height, and depth, I must narrow which end-time themes to treat. It is especially important to have a correct sense of Biblical end-time themes to give a cosmic framework to understand the rise of extremism during the present times of duress. Where and when extremism born of Tension Deficit Disorder comes out of the woodwork; expect two kinds of extreme reaction. First, look for radical liberalism to give birth to forms of fascism.[94] Second, look for radical conservatism to give birth to a rise of fundamentalism where fear, not faith, and law, not gospel, are the dominant notes. Having made these general observations, I will examine seven paradoxes of the end time:

The Paradox of the Present Millennium
The Paradox of the Binding of Satan
The Paradox of the Antichrist
The Paradox of Israel
The Paradox of Life After Death
The Paradox of Hell
The Paradox of Judgment Day

Chapter 9

The Paradox of the Present Millennium

"If you join at eleven o'clock a conversation which began at eight you will often not see the real bearing of what is said. Remarks which seem to you very ordinary will produce laughter or irritation and you will not see why—the very reason of course being that the earlier stages of the conversation have given them a special point."

So writes C.S. Lewis about the importance of the earlier portion of a vital conversation.[95]

Earlier stages of the New Testament enable one to see clearly the nature of the kingdom of God and its relationship to the millennium. *Millennium* is a term derived from two Latin words: *mille*, "a thousand," and *annus*, "a year." When used in theological discussions, the term usually goes back to Revelation 20. Here Scripture talks about a 1,000-year reign. The debate within Christendom is whether the 1,000-year reference is figurative language describing the kingdom of God at work now; or, whether the 1,000-year reference is a literal reference to a 1,000-year visible rule here on earth. Lutherans hold to the former view, the view reflected in the creeds, the view espoused by Augustine, Luther, Aquinas, Calvin, and most of the early church fathers.

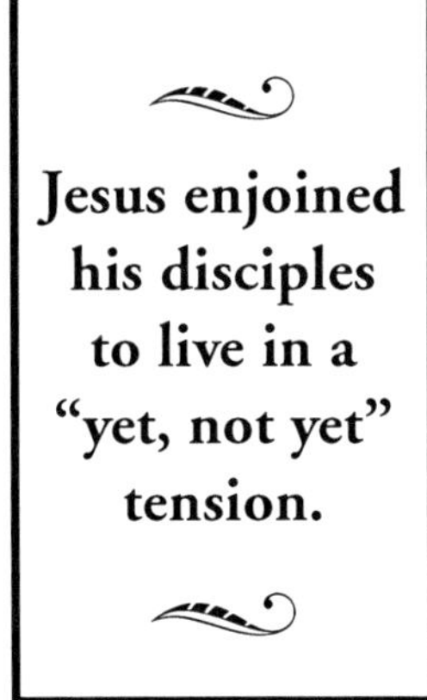

It has been a time-honored rule that a right understanding of what the New Testament sets forth in the first 26 books regarding the kingdom of God will unlock the meaning of what John refers to in the 27th book of the Bible. The "1,000 years" (Revelation 20:4-8) cannot be taken literally any more than the "144,000 ... virgin men who did not soil themselves with women" (Revelation 14:3-4) as the number of people in heaven.[96] The historic way of interpreting this kind of passage is to allow the literal to interpret the figurative, allow the clearer portions of the New Testament to interpret the less clear.

To do otherwise is to fall into the trap of putting the cart before the horse, as do the Jehovah's Witnesses. When they take this tact, they use the less clear to interpret the clearer, they use the figurative to interpret the literal. Furthermore, such a method interprets Revelation not in its native Eastern style but with a foreign linear Western mindset. Rather than seeing Revelation move in the fashion of Hebrew poetry that repeats itself for emphasis and memory purposes, fundamentalists treat Revelation in a strict literalistic, historical chronology. This results in terribly complicated end-time schemes that usually pull the church away from how Jesus comes to us now in time through his gospel. Worse yet, it always has a picture of Jesus locked in one corner of the universe not present with us as both God and man. (Colossians 2:9)[97]

Sacrificed also is the clear New Testament teaching of the "yet, not yet" nature of the kingdom of God. That kingdom that John the Baptizer foretold was at hand. (Matthew 3:2) Jesus also declared that the kingdom of God was at hand. Jesus enjoined his disciples to live in a "yet, not yet" tension. Yes, the kingdom had come in the person of King Jesus but the disciples were, at the same time, instructed to pray, "Thy Kingdom come." (Matthew 6:10) St. Paul reveals that the rule of Christ, the reign of Christ, the kingdom of Christ actually dwells within us through the person of Christ. King Jesus, through the gift of forgiveness of sins and faith, truly dwells within us (Galatians 2:20), as does the Holy Spirit. (1 Corinthians 6:19) This is major kingdom of God stuff! This is huge millennial kingdom rule via the grace of God! To delete this, to minimize this, or to ignore this millennial kingdom rule overlooks the rich resurrection realities that presently comfort and console us.

Sadly, some of the most popular end-time teachers in the last generation have left behind this glorious gospel emphasis in the New Testament. In the 1970s, Hal Lindsey sold 15 million copies of his book, "The Late Great Planet Earth." His book relegated the "yet, not yet" tension to a "not yet" kingdom to come. In the same breath, Lindsey's sensational teachings about a sneak rapture that never did occur moved so opposite of the normal way of faith. Faith says, "I believe so that I see." Hal Lindsey's sign-pointing predictions reversed this with an "I see so that I believe" kind of mentality. On top of this, the sure signs by which Jesus grants us grace, strength, and mercy—word and sacrament—were never part of Lindsey's proclamation.[98]

Similarly, Jerry Jenkins and Tim LaHaye have fallen into the very same ditch as Hal Lindsey. Their *Left Behind* series has sold 67 million copies echoing many of the same failed prophecies of a host of Adventists this past century. Every thirty years or so, when the geopolitical pressures of the world heat up, out of the closet come these escapist prophecies. And what happens? Every time the *Left Behind* people get *left behind.*

The lamentable result of ignoring the "yet, not yet" rule of Christ in the interpretation of the "1,000-year rule" of which John speaks in Revelation 20 is several fold. One, it gives little attention to the heart of the gospel message that justification brings. The fruit of justification stresses a sinner/saint tension as well as the "yet, not yet" tension that the kingdom of Jesus has come yet is also still coming. Even though King Jesus dwells with us and rules here on earth within us, still we pray, "Thy Kingdom come."

Two, the failure to use the paradoxical gospel-vision of victorious martyrs; people who own everything yet nothing, who are at the same time off scouring and yet priests and kings before God, (Revelation 1:7)—the yet—misses a major New Testament theme. The root of this sawed-off view of the kingdom does not believe that King Jesus actually dwells in Christians as the God-man. Thus, there is a double Tension Deficit Disorder.

Three, the view that the rule of Christ is not a present resurrected reality summarized by the figurative language of Revelation 20:5 causes believers to swallow false hopes. I recall personally swallowing Lindsey's sensational version of the end times. I remember looking for the Antichrist to rise out of Europe and Russia, to attack Israel and the Chinese, to send millions of soldiers into the Middle East, and to do battle in Megiddo. Little did I realize I was swallowing camels and straining gnats. I was swallowing a Johnny-come-lately teaching in church history and majoring in minors. I gave minor attention to the theology of Jesus on the cross, his teachings on how he now comes to us, and the greatness of his person.

Over time, I read how the Lindsey-*Left Behind* view really hurt Christians going through an Armageddon experience in the days of Hitler. Back then, Christians were told they would be spared tribulation by the sneak rapture before Hitler could do too much harm. It did not happen. Christians who were counting on this false hope sunk into a heartbroken pessimism when The Third Reich reality came upon them. Because they had abandoned the "yet, not yet" tension of the kingdom of God, of the 1,000 year rule, they did not have a theology of the cross to comfort them but instead were confounded by a theology of glory.

All of this points out the striking difference between a gospel-centered theology and fundamentalism. Fundamentalism began as a good movement around 1912. At that time, a very distinguished group of Bible scholars produced a series of pamphlets on what they called *The Fundamentals, A Testimony of the Truth.* They designed these booklets to uphold the doctrines of verbal inspiration, the vicarious atonement of

Christ, the bodily resurrection, the virgin birth, and the millennium. Much of what *The Fundamentals* put forth was scholarly, salutary, and Scriptural.

What is the difference today between true evangelical theology and fundamentalism? In part, fundamentalism has shifted from fundamentals to the sensational. It is escapism theology that moves away from the message of the cross. The key difference is this: true evangelical theology sees the vital importance of viewing every doctrine in light of the gospel. The Scriptures are not an end in themselves but are given to us for the sake of the gospel. Thus, sound evangelical theology will give high priority to the mighty gospel acts of Holy Baptism, Holy Absolution, and Holy Communion—as well as the message of the cross. It will also not neglect talking about the importance of wrapping up all this in love and humility.

The gospel imparting acts by Jesus of Holy Absolution, Holy Baptism, and Holy Communion (John 20:22-23; Acts 2:38-40; Matthew 26:28) are a key component in the "yet, not yet" life of faith. They are part of the "yet." For fundamentalists, these acts run the way of the law.[99] Suffering a disconnect from the gracious present rule of Christ by faith, from the 1,000 year New Testament last hour, last days millennium, they become externals that offer little internals. For evangelical Christians, these are holy high-octane gospel acts by which Jesus deigns, dines, and descends to friends. Yes, I would agree that there is an element of law in these actions (Newton), but the overwhelming note is gospel (Einstein).

Chapter 10

The Paradox of the Binding of Satan

When Tension Deficit Disorder misses the nature of the rule of Jesus on earth through the church, part of the fallout is to miss the meaning of the binding of Satan. Miss the paradoxical nature of Christ's gracious millennial rule through his church and you will likely overlook this comforting reality.[100] In brief, the New Testament teaches that the devil is simultaneously bound and yet not bound. A full gospel vision of the end times recognizes this paradox. Jesus Christ came into the world as the embodiment of the kingdom of God not only to blind the prince of darkness but to bind Satan as well. (Matthew 12:29)

The New Testament teaches that the devil is simultaneously bound and yet not bound.

This good news reality gets little press among theologians today. Partly, this is the result of Attention Deficit Disorder. The other part is Tension Deficit Disorder. To cure the first, pay close attention to Matthew 12:29. Here Jesus says," Or else how can one enter into a strong man's house, and spoil his goods, except he first bind the strong man? And then he will spoil his house."

The paradox, that Jesus came into the world to blind the prince of darkness, consists in the fact that it was blind rage that drove the devil to have Christ crucified. This was the worst thing the devil could have done from Satan's point of view. Second, the word used in the gospels for the binding [*deo*] of Satan (Matthew 12:29; Mark 3:27) is the root word used in Revelation 20:2 for the binding of Satan for a 1,000 years. Now isn't that a cosmic coincidence?

Here, again, we allow the non-figurative parts of the New Testament to shed light on the figurative parts. When we do, we see the binding of Satan took place during Christ's earthly life through his mighty redemptive deeds. Explicitly, the New Testament tells us that Satan was cast out, judged and defeated at Christ's first advent. (John 12:31, 16:11; 1 John 3:8; Luke 10:18; Hebrews 2:14)[101] Through the suffering of Jesus for our sins, his death on the cross in our place, and his rising from the dead, Christ de-clawed and de-toothed this roaring lion. This good news of Satan's binding is paralleled in Revelation 17:7-13 where the devil is cast out of heaven and is no longer allowed to accuse the saints as he did during Old Testament times. (Zechariah 3; Job 1-2)

When you confess to some Christians that the devil is bound, they give you a look as if to say, "What, you've got to be kidding?" If one walks by mere sight as to what is happening in this wacky wicked world, such skepticism makes sense. Here's the deal. What was hinted at in Revelation 12:9 is made explicit in Revelation 20; namely, that the devil has been bound so that "he could deceive the nations no more." (Revelation 20:3) If we allow the remainder of Scripture rather than mere reasoning to shed light on this binding, and if we understand that the 1,000 years means the New Testament age, the binding of the devil for 1,000 years (Revelation 20:7) makes superb Biblical sense.

How does it make sense? Compared to Old Testament times, the devil's ability to deceive the nations received a substantial blow. At one time, during the age of Noah, the gospel-remnant had dwindled down to eight souls. (1 Peter 3:21) Considering that the world's population at that time may have been far larger than it is today, due to the longevity of the pre-flood span, (Genesis 5) the New Testament biding of Satan squares exceptionally well with the devil's massive disinformation powers in the old eon.

Before the coming of Christ into the flesh, his victory over the temptation of the devil, his casting out of demons hand over fist, the descent of his body and soul into hell to proclaim victory over the devil, (1 Peter 3:18-21) his bodily resurrection, (1 Corinthians 15) and his ascension and coronation, (Ephesians 1:20-23; 4:10) God's salvation was largely limited to believing Jews. While the church today is a shrinking minority in our ever-expanding world, nevertheless, the New Testament binding of Satan allowed the gospel to go to nations in a manner unlike anything during the Old Testament era.[102]

Even though the devil is truly bound—thanks to Christ's decisive victory—Satan is not bound in every sense. The old evil foe still stalketh and walketh about as a roaring lion seeking whom he may devour. (1 Peter 5:7) The fact that the devil's great-in-number filthy crew of fallen cohorts (Ephesians 6:12; Revelation 12:4) also wages war on his behalf makes the Christian ever a person of war as well as a person of peace. The members of God's "yet, not yet" kingdom know that although D-Day occurred, the mopping up operations before V-Day are in full force involving fierce spiritual warfare, major bloody battles, and not just a few Armaggeddons. The fact that the last century witnessed the martyrdom and murder of more than a hundred million Christians as well as the Jewish holocaust of seven million plus the deaths of tens of millions of non-Christians throughout the world might suggest that we may be entering what Scripture knows as "the little season." (Revelation 20:3) When that occurs, it is a biblical sign that all Hades has broken loose, the devil has snapped his chains, and that Christ's glorious, visible return/reappearing is close even as the church is in for a rough ride during the last days of the end times.

Even though the devil may yet be bound—and things get even worse than they were in the last century—we must never get too close to the turf and terrain of the roaring lion. Remember, the devil has his means of disgrace even as God has his means of grace. If we get too close to the devil's lair, be it in the domain of the pornographic or the dominion of drugs, be it the seductive realm of fame or money, be it in any salvation-by-works system or any lawless misadventure, either Satan or one of his filthy crew can devour us. William Hendriksen has worded it well,

> "...within the sphere in which Satan is permitted to exert his influence for evil he rages most furiously. A dog securely bound with a long and heavy chain can do great damage within the circle of his imprisonment. Outside that circle, however, the animal can do no damage and can hurt no one."[103]

Here is the point. The same love of Christ that helps us avoid swallowing camels and straining gnats keeps the devil from swallowing us. How apt are the words of Jude, "Keep yourselves in the paradoxical love of God." (Jude 21, *Free Translation*)

Chapter 11

The Paradox of the Antichrist

With the help of Herman Sasse, we can formulate this paradox in ten words: "The Antichrist is always coming, and he is already here."[104] In light of the "yet, not yet" now, not now tension of the kingdom, such a formulation does not surprise me. The kingdom of the Antichrist runs concurrently with the kingdom of Christ. The "yet, not yet" nature of the Kingdom of Christ and the kingdom of the Antichrist will end only on Judgment Day when the Lord Jesus "shall destroy with the brightness of his coming" (2 Thessalonians 2:8) this "son of perdition." (2 Thessalonians 2:3)

St. Paul, in 2 Thessalonians 2:7, gives the impression that the Antichrist appears in the form of "the man of lawlessness" while 1 John 2:18 gives the impression antichrist will be in the form of many men throughout the New Testament age. Ah, here is another tension. Tension Deficit Disorder is prone to holding one of these truths; a paradoxical faith grasps both. Remember, paradox in service of the gospel combs, collects, and collates all pertinent Scripture.

Throughout history, there have been many attempts to guess the identity of the Antichrist. During World War I, Kaiser Wilhelm was a candidate for this title. During World War II, Mussolini, Hitler, and

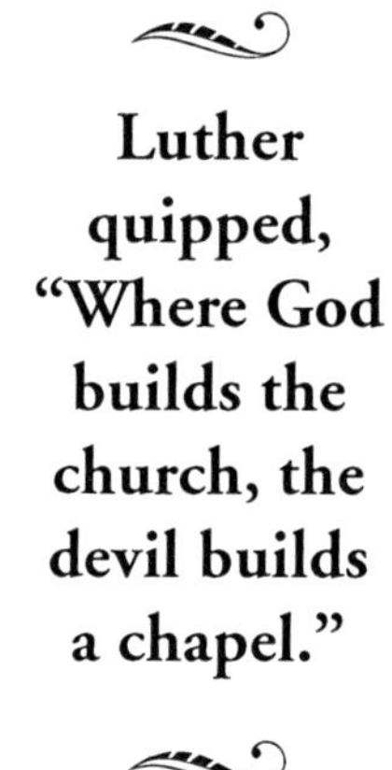

Stalin took their turns as candidates. President John F. Kennedy, Henry Kissinger, and Presidents Jimmy Carter and Ronald Wilson Reagan—Reagan because each of his three names had six letters, ergo, Mr. 666—each got tarred by the antichrist brushes of TDD experts who were straining gnats.

Church history should teach us prophetic reserve. Biblical prophecy regarding the Antichrist should enjoin us to pay close attention to the fact that Antichrist takes his seat "in" the "temple of God," that is, in the church. (2 Thessalonians 2:4) Observing this phenomenon, Luther quipped, "Where God builds the church, the devil builds a chapel."[105]

"Remarkably," writes John Stephenson, "the term *antichrist* itself is absent from the crucial Thessalonians passage, appearing only in the Johannine letters. Here *antichrist* is both a plural and a singular phenomenon, already present and yet to come."[106] With these paradoxical facts, we see that this doctrine on antichrist, in its application and by its very nature, must be more elastic than plastic. It must cover every expression of the antichrist everywhere throughout the whole New Testament age. Hence, the doctrine of the antichrist is a theological shoe that fits all sizes, wherever some substitute gospel replaces God's good news, wherever egotistical people think they can scale their way to heaven through works, or wherever the gospel is some green light to red-light behavior.

Philip Melanchthon identified "the kingdom of Mohammed," with its salvation by works and denial "that men are freely justified before God by faith for Christ's sake," as having the marks of the antichrist.[107] While Melanchthon spotted the fingerprints of the antichrist in the legalism of Mohammed, Luther saw the fingerprints and footprints of the antichrist in the church's leaders of his day. For Luther—whether it was a pope who taught salvation by indulgences, Zwingli's war against the gospel-nature of the Lord's Supper, the work-righteous Turk, or whoever substituted the gospel with some humanistic manifesto or some version of cheap grace—all were in league with the kingdom of the antichrist.

It is important to make two distinctions here. One, we are not judging faith in the heart (*fides qua*) but rather the faith which is confessed (*fides quae*). And any doctrine offered and confessed by any prophet who attempts to water down, sabotage, trim, reduce, obscure, or replace the gospel—especially within the church (2 Thessalonians 2:4)—involves the fumes of antichrist. Therefore, the painful paradox here is that any Christian can easily slip into doing the work of antichrist.[108] Thanks be to God that we are not saved by our perfect faith but by our perfect Savior!

The second distinction is this. No one person and no one institution can exhaust the mystery of the antichrist. While the Antichrist is not Satan himself, he does operate "by the activity of Satan." (2 Thessalonians 2:9) Because of that, Antichrist—under the power of the devil—takes on many disguises, even masquerading as an angel of light. (2 Corinthians 11:14) What pseudo-christ masks and theological toxic admixtures the antichrist might enlist in the future remains to be seen.

No additives to the gospel! That must be our abiding concern if we wish to counter the soul-destroying attacks of the Antichrist. The term *antichrist* carries with it the notion of one who tries to substitute Christ (Greek *anti* means 'in place of') as well as one who opposes Christ. (2 Thessalonians 2:4a) In so far as this is done, antichrist is at work stealing comfort from God's saints and glory from Christ.

A paradoxical vision of the antichrist will help identify the many movements that seek to qualify the radical grace of God through the person of his Son and through the means of grace. A paradoxical vision will not make the myopic mistake of looking for the antichrist in some sole end-times political leader. Furthermore, a paradoxical vision will not overlook the fact that the sinful side of human nature is only too happy to make one's self the center of the universe. Aware of temptations within as well as without, aware of the wider collective character of the antichrist—especially as it operates within the temple of God—alert Christians should seek to let the Word of Christ dwell in them richly. (Colossians 3:16) Knowing that antichrist is always coming and is already here, always seeking to destroy the paradox of justification by grace, is a call to constant readiness in the "yet, not yet" kingdom of God.

Chapter 12

THE PARADOX OF ISRAEL

The paradox in the Bible regarding Israel is important to grasp and hold in tension if one desires to avoid all kinds of theological wild-goose chases. Without a paradoxical vision of the "Israel of God," (Galatians 6:16) one can easily slip into a theology of salvation by race instead of salvation by grace. Christian friends of mine have spoken to me often during past years about "God's chosen people, the Jews," as a blanket statement as if faith in the Messiah did not matter. By speaking in this manner, their view of God's chosen race was one of the flesh rather than faith in Messiah serving as the criterion for being a member of the chosen race with biological bloodline as the bottom line. Ironically, bloodline is what Hitler made as the criterion for his chosen race. Anywhere Hitler goes, I go the opposite way.

Salvation by bloodline is a wrong position in light of justification by grace through faith in Messiah Jesus, but it is also wrong from another historical point of view. Recall how King David came from, in part, a Gentile bloodline. (Ruth 1:5; 4:21,22) To disregard this fact would be plain ruthless.

Perhaps it is time to spell out the paradox regarding Israel. The string of evangelical theology's bow stretches this way: all of Israel will

be saved and not all of Israel will be saved. St. Paul presents this paradox in Romans 9-11. On the one hand, Paul writes, "All Israel will be saved." (Romans 11:26) On the other hand, he also writes, "Only a remnant will be saved." (Romans 9:27) Such a flexing of the theological bow begs a sort of C.S. Lewis question, "In what sense is Paul speaking when he sets up each of these truths?"

This paradox distressed the apostle Paul. As a result, he wrote, "I have great heaviness and continual sorrow in my heart. For I could wish that myself were accursed from Christ for my brethren, my kinsmen according to the flesh." (Romans 9:2-3) Luther's comment about this kind of thinking is itself paradoxical, "It seems incredible that a man would desire to be damned in order that the damned might be saved."[109] Of course, this was precisely the path Jesus took for all mankind. (Matthew 27:46)[110]

The paradox that all of Israel will be saved and not all of Israel will be saved shows us that it is distinction time. There is an Israel within Israel. Paradoxically, this remnant is larger in number than the biological fabric of Israel itself. It is greater in number for Messiah's vineyard includes large grafted/living branches. (Romans 11:13-26) These adopted branches, to use the prophetic words of the Messiah, will come from "the east and west, and shall sit down with Abraham, and Isaac, and Jacob, in the kingdom of heaven." (Matthew 8:11)

God gives each of us the paradox of Israel to teach us that God's Israel is a spiritual Israel. Unless we see this vision clearly, we are subject to salvation by bloodline, false prophecies of sneak raptures, and a theology that focuses on fringes. More than thirty years ago, Hal Lindsey's *The Late Great Planet Earth* told people, "don't expect to be around much longer." That warning evolved into the notion that the rapture is about to occur and the Russian forces of God are about to descend upon the nation of Israel.[111] With maps, arrows, and diagrams he drew up a wild land-centered scenario. With a recklessness born of Tension Deficit Disorder and devoid of the paradoxical vision that Paul spoke about in Romans 9-11, Lindsey made a slew of predictions that missed the mark.

Not only was Hal Lindsey's land-centered view proven wrong over time, but he tragically diverted millions of people from seeing the real Israel of God. (Galatians 6:16; 1 Peter 2:9) The real Israel of God, according to the Bible, is a creation by God through the Red Sea miracle of baptism. Through the paradoxical gospel event of baptism, one becomes a child of God by faith in Jesus the Messiah. (Galatians 3:26-27) This awesome act creates a fundamental Jewish-Gentile solidarity in God's Israel, the church. (Galatians 3:28) Added to this good news is the fact that via the grace of God in baptism, when we "put on Messiah" (3:27), we simultaneously become part of Abraham's seed. (3:29) Along with this, we are actually incorporated into the very body of the Messiah who is not bound by time, space or race. (1 Corinthians 12:13) That good news should give Christians warm chills.

As indicated earlier, like many Christians, I became enamored with Hal Lindsey's Johnny-come-lately theological TDD views. I had just crawled out of a far left theological ditch only to stagger into the opposite ditch of fundamentalism. I went from swallowing camels, a cheap grace kind of theology, to straining gnats, a different kind of cheap grace theology minus any means of grace emphasis. I was the peasant drunk. At the first booze trough, credentialed professors taught me "Doubt is the first step of faith." By itself, that phrase suffers TDD. A more balanced Biblical view recognizes that good doubt and bad doubt can exist simultaneously. Wisdom discerns the difference.

Jesus demonstrated a lot of sanctified skepticism in his day when it came to embracing dogma that departed from the law and gospel of the Torah or failed to take seriously the prophets. On the one hand, Jesus never doubted the will of the Father. (Hebrews 4:15) On the other hand, history's most influential teacher demonstrated deep doubt toward many of the teachings of the Scribes, Sadducees, and Pharisees. These men became experts in straining gnats. They took God's good law and added to it ridiculous nitpicking rules and regulations that ran opposite of the spirit of Yahweh. They declared it evil for a poor paralyzed man to be healed on the Sabbath. Inflexible human ritual trumped God's flexible compassion. (Matthew 12:7)

After I had been in and then out of the ditch on the far left, it took me a good number of years to crawl fully out of the ditch on the right. Low-octane gospel marked each ditch. In the ditch on the left, the person and work of Jesus was minimized so that he was pretty much just one Savior among many. In the other ditch, the spectacular work of Jesus on the cross and the awesome works through his sacraments were sacrificed for maps, charts, and human predictions that went beyond the Bible. In the first ditch, so many of my professors spent time ditching the virgin birth and other miracles. In the second ditch, the theological teachers ditched key arms of the distribution center of grace that is Jesus. A brother in the faith wrote to me in 1996 how he also too took a long time to get rid of the TDD view of the *Late Great Planet Earth.* He wrote:

> About six years ago, God changed my understanding of eschatology from a view which focused on the nation of Israel as central to end-time events to one which sees Christ and the promise of His return as central. This change came as I read Luther and learned from him that all doctrine is rightly understood when Christ is at the center, and that any doctrinal interpretation which causes people to look hopefully, to any source other than Christ is a false interpretation. When I realized this, I stopped looking for a temple built in Jerusalem and for other events relating to the nation of Israel, and now look instead for the return of the Savior Jesus Christ.[112]

Chapter 13

The Paradox of Life After Death

Years ago, when I was first serving as a pastor, I recall a rather irritated member of the congregation speaking to me after a church service. He took issue with an assertion I made in the sermon. "Pastor," he said, "You had it all wrong in the sermon today. When we die, we do not go to heaven. That does not take place until Judgment Day when we are raised from the dead."

This saint was partly right. He was latching on to the truth of St. Augustine that the cemeteries are dormitories for the dead. Rather, they are dormitories for the bodies of the saints who are living in heaven. That is the good news tension.

I felt sorry for this saint. For years he had been living, believing, and laboring under false belief thinking that at the point of death a Christian dies, his or her body rots, and that's it until the second coming. The problem here is lack of a fuller gospel vision, a lack of paradoxical vision that sees a most comforting dimension of death for the Christian. Jesus expressed this paradox to Martha at the death of her brother, Lazarus. It is a paradox that issues from the paradox *Condescendit nobis Deus, ut nos consurgamus* (God condescends to us so that we rise with Him."[113] What is this paradox? It is this paradox from the Lord of life: "I am the resurrection, and the life: he

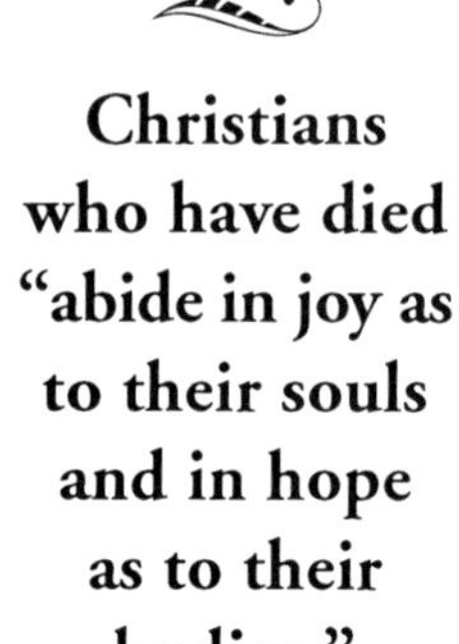

that believeth in me, though he were dead, yet shall he live" (John 11:25).[114]

The Lutheran Agenda fashions this paradox in a beautiful manner when it speaks of Christians who have died as ones who "abide in joy as to their souls and in hope as to their bodies."[115] Is there a Biblical basis to teach that the moment a Christian dies, his or her spirit or soul goes to heaven, that a personal identity remains intact between death and the bodily resurrection? In other words, is there an intermediate state between death and bodily resurrection?

So clear is the New Testament's witness to the reality of the intermediate state that one is amazed when Christians question the "yet, not yet" dimensions of the "even though we die, yet shall we live" promise of our Lord. It was this word that Jesus spoke plainly to the repentant thief who hung beside him on a cross that same Good Friday. (Luke 23:43) Jesus confirms that the soul does not die with the body when he cries out in victory, "Father, into thy hands I commend my spirit." (Luke 23:46) Stephen, a post-Pentecost follower of Jesus, also expressed the highest of hopes of a direct encounter with the Lord upon death, exclaiming, "Lord Jesus, receive my spirit." (Acts 7:59)[116]

Throughout the Bible as a whole, we see the holy writers speaking of the departed faithful as existing in a conscious state, (Revelation 6:9-11; 7:9-10, 14-15) a blessed state, (Psalm 73:24-26) and immediate paradise upon death. (Luke 23:43) In Philippians 1:21-23, St. Paul speaks of death for the Christian as resulting in a substantial upgrade from this present life. Implied is a life, to use the literal words of St. Paul, which is "very much better!" The story of the believing beggar who dies and yet goes to heaven (Luke 16:23) resounds with a loud, echoing Amen to the blessed end that awaits the believer in Christ.

Granted, one can overplay this good news emphasis and suffer TDD from the opposite side of the spectrum. There remains the "not yet" side of the new "yet." Yes, upon death the spirit of the Christian immediately goes to heaven, yet the full consummation awaits. There is the grim element of the graveside. There is the decaying body that is lifeless. There is painful separation from loved ones. There is the waiting for the spirit in paradise to join with the glorified body at the end of history.

I suspect one of the reasons Christians cite as a basis for by-passing the Biblical teaching that "to be absent from the body is to be present with the Lord," (2 Corinthians 5:8) resides in a one-sided emphasis upon the Biblical passages that set forth what is known as "soul-sleep." For example, St. Paul writes to the Thessalonians, "But I would not have you to be ignorant, brothers, concerning them who are asleep that ye sorrow not even as others who have no hope." (1 Thessalonians 4:13)

No doubt about it, Scripture in its typically wonderful way is beautifully balanced, carefully chiseled, and avoids TDD. Scripture does speak of those who die in Jesus as sleeping. However, at the same time it speaks of the spirits of the saints in paradise.

Luther gives us the right picture of soul sleep in his lectures on Genesis. Speaking about the deaths of the patriarchs of the Old Testament, Luther describes how the believer who has died is asleep and yet awake. (As an aside, according to Scripture, unbelievers are people who are awake, yet asleep, alive yet dead.) (Ephesians 5:14; 2:1) Writing in his typically colorful paradoxical manner, Luther the Reformer describes the dialectic of being asleep yet awake:

> Nevertheless, there is a difference between the sleep or rest of this life and that of the future life. For toward night a person who has become exhausted by his daily labor in this life enters into his chamber of peace, as it were, to sleep there; and during this night he enjoys rest and has no knowledge whatever of any evil caused either by fire or murder. But the soul does sleep in the same manner. It is awake. It experiences visions and the discourses of the angels and of God. Therefore the sleep in the future life is deeper than it is in this life. Nevertheless, the soul lives before God .... Nevertheless, God preserves the waking soul. Thus God is able to awaken Elijah, Moses, etc., and so to control them that they live. But how? We do not know.[117]

Chapter 14

The Paradox of Hell

At the end of his *Doctrinal Theology of The Evangelical Lutheran Church*, Heinrich Schmid discusses matters pertaining to eternal damnation and eternal life. After quoting a number of church fathers on these two eschatological subjects, he concluded his lengthy, dogmatic text with a most memorable anecdote. He wrote about one of the ancients who asked what books he used in his daily study of God's Word. The ancient responded that he studied every day a book with three pages, one red, one black, and one white. On the red page, he read of our Lord's suffering and death. On the black page, he read about the torments of the lost. On the white page, he studied the joys of those in the church above. From his study, he derived more comfort and profit than if he were to ponder all the books of the philosophers.[118]

It is the second page of this three-page book that we hear so little about today. Hell is a subject that seems to have just vanished. Martin Marty has observed that "hell disappeared and no one noticed."[119] One hears little about it from today's "power of positive thinking" pulpits. Consequently, when there is such a vacuum, false views rush in to fill the void.

Even though Jesus talked about hell three times more than he did about heaven, most churches censor this teaching today. It is another side of Tension Deficit Disorder. The doctrine of hell—eternal separation from God through unbelief in the Savior of the world—needs resurrection. To minimize hell is to minimize heaven, the hellish suffering of Jesus on the cross, the importance of faith and love, and the horror of sin and evil. While his English grammar was not perfect, Billy Sunday's theology was on target when he said, "If there ain't no hell, there ain't no heaven." We need this strong word of law for the sake of the gospel lest universalism and the deadly apathy that comes with it overtake us. Universalism is the deadly notion that all people will be saved regardless of what they believe.

During the 1980s, I encountered universalism firsthand when I attended a lecture at Tulane University where the famous theologian, Jurgen Moltmann, was delivering a lecture on Romans 9 through 11. Using a carefully reasoned but eclectic dialectic, Moltmann made his case on less than the whole of Scripture. He stated that God justified the whole world declaring it not guilty, which is true enough. However, he went on to argue that, therefore, all people will be saved whether they believe or not, which is very false. Moltmann's mistake was this; he went from universal justification and universal grace—Jesus died for all—to universalism when he declared that all will be saved. (TDD) While Jesus did die for all sin and all sinners, (2 Corinthians 5:15) and God has declared the whole world not guilty, (2 Corinthians 5:19) it remains "he that believeth not the Son shall not see life; but the wrath of God abideth on him." (John 3:36)

I can summarize Moltmann's problem in three words: Tension Deficit Disorder. After his lecture, I politely asked him two questions during the open forum setting. First, I asked him if he thought all people would be saved.

He said, "Yes."

Then I asked him a more pointed question, "Would an unrepentant Adolph Hitler also be saved?"

That question evoked a testy response, "Why do all you Southern theologians think I am a universalist?"

"Because you are," I said.

Sensing the tension in the auditorium created by his TDD position, the professor gave a very clever response to assuage some of the rising anger due to his hedging. He said, "If it were up to me, Adoph Hitler would not be in heaven. But God's grace is greater than mine."

Moltmann's answer, though shrewd enough to avoid a brouhaha, still suffered Tension Deficit Disorder. The gospel is indeed the good news that Jesus died for all. It is also the good news that God has declared the whole world not guilty for the sake of his dear Son. Finally, it is also the good news that the gospel works saving faith and love within the hearts of those who are saved. Without this good news, there is only bad news for humanity.[120]

T.S. Eliot said if we rid the doctrine of the final judgment in favor of universalism, we convert God into a Santa Claus who declares, "Everybody shall have toys and be glad."[121] Worse yet, it is a fact that the less we say about hell the more hell on earth we will have. One wonders what would happen if terrorists, rapists, sexual perverts, porno kings, drug lords, the Hitlers, the Stalins, and other extreme degenerates would hear the truth that there are degrees of hell for the notorious predator. (Matthew 11:22-24) Might not that knowledge serve as a sharp surgical procedure of the law to curb and crush a measure of their arrogance? Might it not, in some cases, serve as a mirror bright enough to bring their inbred sins to light? (Romans 3:20) If the law of God is about the love of God, (Romans 13:10) is it loving to reduce the straight edge of God's law that reveals the crookedness of mankind?

I must admit to you that the doctrine of hell does trouble me. I think it also troubles most Christians. At the same time, it troubles me far more not to have the doctrine of hell. Once again, Christians are called to live with tension. Not to live in tension is to slip into extremes, eliminate the need for faith, and bite into fruit from the Tree of Knowledge of Good and Evil.

I vigorously work to make the gospel the paramount note of my preaching, teaching, and life. As I do so, I see a definite need for the doctrine of hell. I see it from the perch and perspective of having suffered severely as a child. Having grown up in a family where my siblings and I were beaten badly by a lawless, tyrannical, alcoholic father—beaten within an inch of our lives—it frightens me to think about a world in which there is no bar of justice such as the doctrine of hell. Without the doctrine of hell, my father would have had no moral brakes to stop him from doing the unthinkable. I can say without a doubt that the doctrine of hell probably kept our father from murdering us. I can say this as one who forgave my father and holds no grudges toward him, only deep lament for his cruelties.

Often, people who have a philosophical problem with hell have not been under the brutal boot of a lawless tyrant. They have not been truly oppressed, beaten, and bloodied by someone who swallows camels and strains gnats. They have not suffered deep physical pain, degradation, and humiliation. Nor have they ever sensed how the doctrine of hell is a curb in numerous instances in keeping people from terrorizing others with total impunity of the consequences. Let me give you a very real example of the curbing power of the doctrine of hell from a true to life story.

As a pastor, I went many years ago to the home of a church member. It was a Sunday afternoon. The wife was afraid to return home. The night before, her deranged husband tortured her physically and even burned her with a hot lamp. He smashed all of her heirlooms that were in the house. For hours, he cursed at her, threatened her, pulled her hair, abused her, and raved bloody murder. All this he did while sober. It was a classic case of him swallowing camels with his reckless behavior and then acting as if he were some morally superior ethical being who could strain gnats. Fearful for the woman's well-being, I accompanied her to the house and tried to talk some sense into the jerk. In reality, the guy was performing a masterful bit of acting in an effort to feign mental illness in order to obtain a lucrative early retirement package from his employer so that he could then travel around the world.

As she and I walked into the woman's home, we quickly noticed that her husband was lying down on the couch. His arms stretched out in a crucifix fashion. His tongue hung out of his mouth. Empty pill bottles were strewn around. It looked as if he might have taken an overdose of pills. Quickly, I ran up to the man and felt for his jugular vein. His pulse was still throbbing. The next instant I raced to a phone and dialed 9-1-1. Suddenly, the man jumped up from the couch and began screaming, cursing in a vile manner, and thundering maledictions. He was double furious now. His cruel tricks performed earlier upon his battered, beleaguered wife had backfired to the point that she had brought home the preacher to witness his bizarre antics.

The evil this man manifested was pernicious, palpable, and dangerous. So vile and vicious were his verbal assaults that I did something that I have never repeated during my 27 years as a pastor. I screamed at this man at the top of my lungs.

"Clark, you are going to go to the place were the worm does not die and the fire is not quenched," I shouted. "You will be a loathsome object of God's wrath forever. You will stink for all eternity. You will suffer for all eternity. You will be in utter agony for all eternity. Furthermore, you will suffer far worse in hell than most people will.

"Jesus taught about degrees of hell and you are bucking for one of the lowest spots in hell," I continued to yell. "Heck, you may even earn the dishonor to buddy up with Hitler, Stalin, and all the other perverse degenerates.

"Clark, you better love heat, you better love excruciating pain, you better love to smell like sulfur and stench, look like maggots, and you better expect the full force of the holy wrath of the Lamb," I ranted on. "Unless you repent, turn away from your wicked selfish stinking lousy putrid sin, you will burn for all eternity!"

The man who had tortured his wife all night the evening before turned stone silent after the full fury of God's law came from my mouth and into his ears. Upon hearing my non-stop counter response, Clark backed up about twelve steps and then crouched in a corner without uttering a single word.

By this time, police began to swarm around the house because the man was known to have more guns in his home than the movie character Rambo. The police burst into the house and brought an added measure of human law into the room. I was fortunate that they did not try to arrest me for my impassioned sermon on hell and brimstone.

Something happened at Clark's home that I did not quite expect. My goal simply was to get him to back off from hurting his wife. She later told me that the strong word of law had cut through Clark's bluster and bravado. It sobered him spiritually. It worked on his soul. It was the beginning of a road that enabled him to see his wicked rampages for what they were, brought him to confess his sins, brought him to receive Christ's forgiveness, and brought him to accept Christ's love. That sermon literally changed that man's life. The strong word of law that I imparted started him on the road to repentance and sparked a change in Clark's life. I am convinced that the Holy Spirit, through the stern law of Isaiah 66 that I applied vigorously that day, began a law-gospel surgery on this previously tyrant of a husband. By the way, I was able to quote that passage with force and fury on that particular day because it was the appointed Old Testament reading for Lord's Day divine service. Many TDD churches have removed that kind of reading from their lectionaries. I am sure glad it remains in our church. We need a balance between clean law and comforting gospel, with the gospel always the dominant note as we comfort the afflicted and afflict the comfortable.

Another form of Tension Deficit Disorder today is annihilationism. Annihilationism is a view that those who end up in hell through unbelief that rejects God's greatest gift—the forgiveness, life, and salvation of Jesus—will pass out of existence upon death. Now, had I threatened Clark with annihilationism, I do not think that would have dented his evil armor. Rather than exhibiting the sharp teeth of God's law, annihilationism acts more like dull dentures. It is a dull doctrine that does not cut through the thick walls of evil to prepare the way for the good news of the gospel. At best, it is a high-powered theological peashooter.

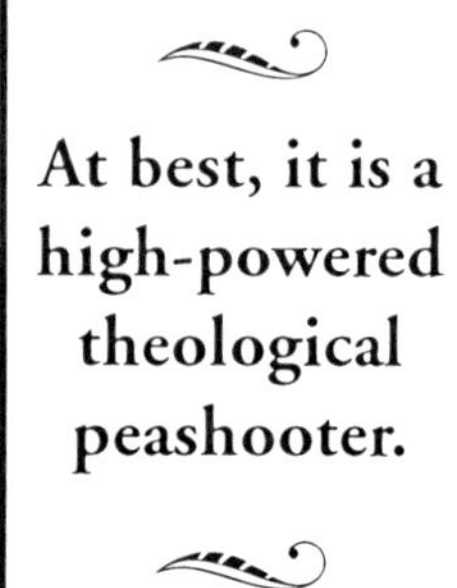

Throughout the ages, groups as far ranging as the Jehovah's Witnesses and Zwinglian Anabaptists and even somewhat conservative Biblical scholars such as Clark Pinnock and John Stott have advanced this well-meaning but dangerous nihilistic doctrine. Francis Pieper writes:

> "The objections raised in all ages to the endlessness of the infernal punishment are understandable; for the thought of a never-ending agony of rational beings, fully realizing their distressing plight, is so appalling that it exceeds comprehension."[122]

The logical reality is this: Remove the doctrine of hell and there is no need for faith, hope, and love. If there is no hell in the manner as Christ taught it, then history's most influential person for the good was a liar, scoundrel, and charlatan. Jesus spoke about hell in such a way that he left no doubt that it is a place of eternal weeping and gnashing of teeth. (Matthew 8:12; 13:42,50; 22:13; 24:51; 25:30-46) Reject what Jesus says about hell and one will contribute unwittingly to a lot more pain here on earth. Granted, spiritual masochists have abused the doctrine of hell throughout the ages. However, whenever it is rightly used it will serve as a stern word of law for the sake of the gospel. Rightly used, it curbs a tremendous amount of murder and mayhem, violence and viciousness, lawlessness and lovelessness.

Let me add one more paradox about hell. This paradox comes from C.S. Lewis. Dr. Francis Rossow amplifies it:

> "The doors of hell are, first of all, locked from the inside—only afterwards locked also from the outside. To people unable to say to God, 'Thy will be done,' God ultimately and reluctantly replies, 'Thy will be done'—and, of course, that's the hell of it."[123]

Chapter 15

The Paradox of Judgment Day

The Athanasian Creed, one of the three great ecumenical creeds, concludes with these sobering words, "And they that have done good shall go into life everlasting; and they that have done evil, into everlasting fire." That, by the way, was the universal (catholic) accepted position of the early church. At first glance, these words seem to run at variance with the paradoxical, central doctrine of justification by grace through faith in Jesus apart from the works of the law. (Romans 3:28) And yet, the same apostle who eloquently wrote about salvation by grace in Ephesians 2:8,9 also wrote, "For we must all appear before the judgment seat of Christ; that every one may receive the things done in his body, according to that he hath done, whether it be good or bad." (2 Corinthians 5:10)[124]

Through the law-gospel lenses of Scripture, a paradox regarding our works as the norm on Judgment Day is unmistakable. This is half of the formulation we must hold in tension lest we go too far toward the camp of legalism. Scripture does teach that on Judgment Day Christians will be judged according to their works. A very enlightening section of Scripture that presents this paradox is the account of Judgment Day given to us by Matthew in his gospel. (Matthew 25:31-46)[125]

In this account, Jesus addresses his disciples on the Mount of Olives shortly before his suffering, death, and bodily resurrection. He tells them that one day he will visibly return in glory to judge all the nations. (Matthew 25:32) Noteworthy is the fact that there is not the slightest hint of a sneak rapture. On the contrary, Jesus presents a scenario in which "every eye will see him." (Revelation 1:7)[126] When he comes, all his holy angels will be with him. On that day, humanity will divide into two camps: goats and sheep, unbelievers and believers, the damned and the redeemed.

To the sheep, Jesus as King speaks words of salvation by grace, "Come, ye blessed of my Father, inherit the kingdom prepared for you from the foundation of the world." (Matthew 25:34) Remember, paradox always scans the whole of Scripture before pronouncement. It does, as Luther says, shake the whole tree of Scripture to get the fullest harvest from God's Word on any given issue. In Matthew's account of Judgment Day, we see words of gospel coming before words of judgment with regard to God's elect, the sheep, the believers in Christ. God's gracious initiative precedes his grace-filled judgment.

What does Jesus say to his sheep on Judgment Day? What is the nature of the judgment by the King of Kings? It is a joyful judgment of mercy. They are judged solely according to the works they have done in helping the hungry and thirsty brethren, in ministering to fellow Christians who were strangers, naked, and in prison. Remember, they are doing the good works that the Holy Spirit, through the gospel, moves them to do by the merit of Christ and the mercy of the Father! (Philippians 1:6) To put it another way, the Triune God, the God of all grace, is judging them and rewarding them solely for the good works that he works through them. Talk about grace upon grace upon grace!

Observe carefully. Watch out for ADD—Attention Deficit Disorder. Look out for TDD—Tension Deficit Disorder. See how the believers in Christ are judged according to their works but are not saved by them. This is a huge difference! Mark Twain said there is a world of difference between lightning and the lightning bug. Equally true, there is a universe of difference between being judged by one's good works versus being saved by them. The former is Scriptural; the latter is raw heresy changing Christianity to the likes of every other world religion which ends up being man-centered, legalistic, work-righteous gnat straining.

Thus, we see Christians will be judged according to their works—their good works, the good works Jesus has worked in them—which really are the works of Christ through the gospel. Now that is good news! However, there is even more good news yet to come. Notice that in this account in Matthew not a single sin is mentioned or brought up against the sheep, the believers in Christ. Why? Paul tells us, "There is therefore now no condemnation to them who are in Christ Jesus." (Romans 8:1) For believers, those on Christ's right hand, their evil works will not even be brought up on Judgment Day. Their sins have been cast into the depths of the sea. (Micah 7:19)

This then is the picture; believers in Christ will be judged only on the basis of the good works that God works in them. Second, we believers will not be judged on the basis of our evil works in any shape or form. Splicing together all the strands of the gospel on this matter, a most comforting preview of coming attractions emerges for the children of God. The unbeliever, on the other hand, who lives by the law will die by the law eternally. (Matthew 25:46a; Galatians 3:10) Those who rejected the gospel of Christ will hear the law from him: "Ye gave me not meat (law); ye gave me no drink (law); ye did not cloth me (law); ye did not visit me (law); ye did not minister unto me (law)!" (Matthew 25:43-44)

A close examination of this Judgment Day text is a reminder to the Christian that there is no room for sloth or synergism. Although we are not justified by works, a justified man works. (Ephesians 2:8-10) This powerful end-time narrative helps us to accent the human response to God's goodness without reducing the complete gift that is the nature of salvation. Says Köberle:

> "So here theology is again forced to the paradoxical statement that the activity of sanctification, because it is a fruit of the tree of faith, does not give us any claim on God, nor any occasion for self praise (1 Corinthians 3:6 seq.), but that its omission destroys both the fruit and the root. The tree that cannot grow dies."[127]

See the balance? Behold the tension! Avoid straining gnats and swallowing camels. Only the paradoxical gospel can take one on the true golden middle path.

The paradox of Judgment Day, namely that we will be judged and we will not be judged, enables the Christian to see the nimbleness of Scripture as one more glorious facet of the gospel. Because of the good news of Christ's gifts of salvation—forgiveness of sins, perfective obedience, life, love, and righteousness—we will be judged in mercy, not wrath. We will be judged, yes; condemned, no. Consequently, the Christian hope is not confidence that we will escape Judgment Day, but confidence for Judgment Day. Using the poetic nature of the Greek original, we will have *parresia* for the *parousia*, boldness for Christ's second coming.

Chapter 16

Where the Rubber Hits the Road

One of my favorite movies is the 1985 release called "Witness." It stars Harrison Ford who plays a tough Philadelphia detective. When a young Amish woman and her son witness the murder of an undercover narcotics agent, detective John Book (Ford) must be their savior. The result is an action-packed movie that depicts the clash of two cultures; the Amish way of life versus the need for the use of force in the rough law-and-order lifestyle of John Book. In a way, the movie deals with the tension between Romans 12:19 of never taking personal revenge and Romans 13:1-7, where God grants the government authority to use force to punish and subdue evildoers. (Romans 13:4)

In the movie, there is a critical moment where Ford's character discovers that his boss is up to his neck in the world of narcotics. It is his boss who has put a hit—issued a contract for murder—on Book as well as others. By way of a phone call, John Book confronts his crooked boss. He asks him, "Remember what you used to say about cops gone bad?" He then added the lie, "You used to say 'they lost the meaning.' "

It is so easy for people as well as church bodies to lose the meaning. The great Lutheran question always is: What does this mean? Luther, an Augustinian monk, took his cue from the North African theologian.

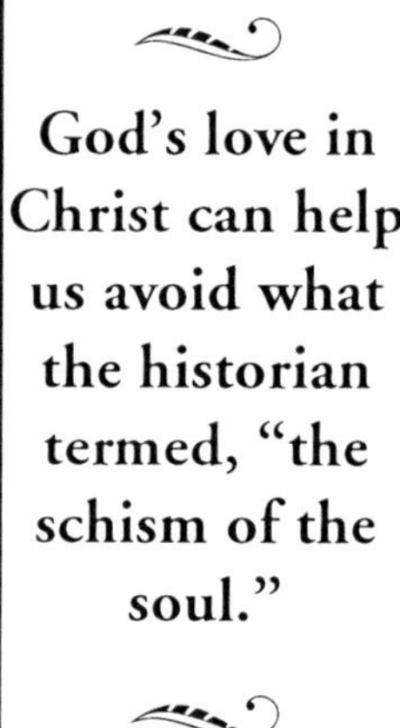

Augustine said that the key to breaking the back of a tough issue was through the asking of good questions.

For church bodies today, the key question is: What is the essence of one's heritage? The thesis of this book has been to demonstrate that the heart of Christianity is its paradoxical gospel. Moreover, this paradoxical gospel is the one true religion that can help people avoid swallowing camels or straining gnats. Throughout Christendom, we see church bodies being seduced by extremes; swallowing camels or straining gnats of lawlessness and legalism, Epicureanism and Asceticism.

Only the good news of God's love in Christ can help us avoid what the historian termed, "the schism of the soul." English historian Arnold Joseph Toynbee used that term in the last century to describe how the Western world was drifting toward extremes as people, institutions, and traditions became unhinged from core beliefs. While Toynbee did not footnote this as a drift from the paradoxical gospel—the roots—he did recognize that it was drifting away from the fruits of Christianity. Alert Christians see that the noblest traditions of the West flow from the paradoxes of the Christian faith and love of Christ, who is the absolute paradox.

Take, for example, the Marshall Plan that followed World War II. The United States gave millions of dollars to help our wartime enemies rebuild their nations. Such a mindset you will never find in any culture unless the profound love of the absolute paradox and his teachings permeate a critical mass who collectively begin to think in such a manner. Abraham Lincoln said that one gets rid of an enemy by turning him into a friend. Lincoln, the one-time agnostic, could not have thought that way apart from the Holy Spirit through the paradoxical gospel revealing the wisdom of such a disposition.

Arguably, the best-selling book in the field of leadership during 2001 was Jim Collin's *Good to Great.*[129] What is most striking about this book and its author is his paradoxical approach to understanding greatness. After years of passionate, detailed, empirical research with a top-notch think tank team, Collins identified a very select group from thousands of major companies. He lists only eleven companies that, in his estimation, had gone from good to great. Intriguing are Collin's derived principles gained from his careful research as to what lifts a company from good to great. In short, they breathe the breath of paradox.

Collin's description of Kimberly-Clark, Inc., is a classic example of a company willing to lose its life in order to regain it. To use Collin's words, at a crucial time in that company's history, Kimberly-Clark officials showed a "willingness to confront brutal facts." They were willing to cut off their right hand if that was what prevented them from making necessary changes. (Matthew 5:30) Cutting off their so-called right hand—by selling all their paper mills—Kimberly-Clark executives freed the company's energies to go from good to great.[130] This Sermon on the Mount allusion and Collin's conclusion at the core speak the same truth. While Jesus was using this metaphor to illustrate the concept of exercising the gift of robust repentance in the kingdom of God, Collins uses it as an argument for necessary change within the business world.

Dr. Kenneth Cooper, a physician, has written a book titled *Can Stress Heal?*[131] In the book, he talks about the importance of healthy sleep, aerobic physical exercise, and other salutary habits. Guess what is number one on his list in terms of good health? Step number one is "Assume a Paradoxical Mind-Set." For example, Dr. Cooper enjoins people to see a crisis as not all bad, but rather as something that is partly good and partly bad at the same time.

The very freedom we have in the United States of America was predicated upon a people who would be willing to demonstrate a paradoxical mindset. They would need to be a citizenry that stood steadfast against the extreme of anarchy as well as the extreme of totalitarian rule. Something would need to be in the water whetting their appetite to think this way. Fortunately, men like James Madison, George Washington, Alexander Hamilton, and even the quasi-deist Thomas Jefferson were steeped in the

Scriptures and impacted by the paradoxical natures of Moses, Solomon, and Jesus.[132] At times, these men did indeed suffer from Tension Deficit Disorder. Yet, even then, Hamilton, the strong central government advocate, would balance out Jefferson, the strong states' rights cheerleader, with Washington acting as the fulcrum for these two headstrong savants. Keep in mind that George Washington drew deeply from his faith in Christ and constant study of the Bible to navigate a course that sought to avoid extremes.[133]

What about mainline Christianity? I believe America is in a severe crisis because church leaders are having a terrible time steering between the Scylla of lawlessness and the Charybdis of legalism. In Europe, the church has long been on life support. The reason Hitler came to power in Germany was that the churches, even back then, were dwindling, dividing, and divorcing themselves from a true gospel-centered theology. Swapping their evangelical paradoxical birthright for theological caprice the slopes would be greased for a series of proxy messiahs. With a severe theological vacuum present, a string of small Hitlers and healers would give way to a big Hitler. "Heal us Hitler" became a salutation, mantra, and prayer by millions of Germans.[134]

To give the readers of this book some thought for food, I would like to wrestle with two hot potato items within American Christianity. They are matters in which Tension Deficit Disorder can take over in a hurry. One is the issue of women's ordination. The other is the issue of what we refer to as either close Communion or closed Communion. Church bodies that swing too wide or too narrow on either of these issues will end up losing a gospel-centered identity. If the historic core of the holy Christian church and the avoidance of extremism is not important to you, I am surprised that you have already read this much of my book. However, if the essence of the Christian faith and the good news of God's love in Christ are important to you, I hope that you will grapple with these two matters. At the end of the day, it is my contention that every Christian must know where to draw his or her theological lines. God willing, we will draw them together in the proper places for the sake of the gospel.

This brings me to a crucial point; to know the score one must know the core. What really is the core of the gospel? Let me turn to two poets of paradox. First, listen to Adoph Köberle who wrote, "The essence of the gospel may be described in two statements: God in Christ seeks the lost through His Word, and quickens the dead."[135] Martin Luther gives us another helpful snapshot:

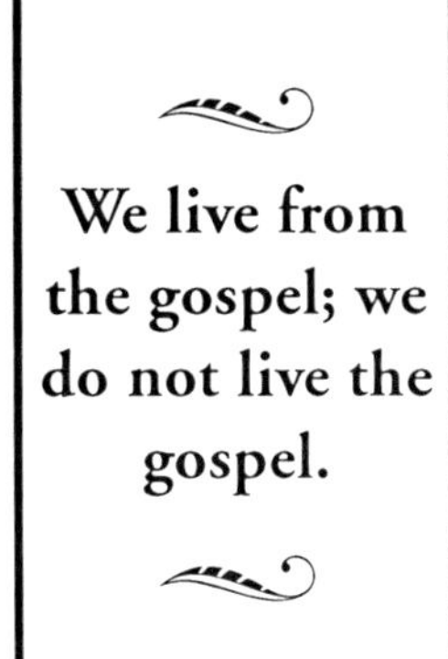

> If you ask: What is the gospel? No better answer can we find than these words of the New Testament: Christ gave His body and shed His blood for us for the forgiveness of sins. This alone is to be preached to Christians, impressed upon them, and faithfully commended to them for constant meditation.[136]

In a broad sense, the gospel involves sin and grace. This too is a tension. We must proclaim the law for the sake of the gospel and to make hearts ready for the gospel. Where there is a sense of sin, the gospel can do its proper work of granting forgiveness, life, and salvation. While Lutherans at times use the gospel to include the law, we generally avoid using *law* as a gospel term. Certainly, there is an exception in the case of Psalm 1, Psalm 119, and other Hebrew Scriptures where the word for law (*Torah*) includes elements of law and gospel. The Torah, the first five books of the Hebrew Scriptures, reveals what we are to do and not to do, and at the same time, reveals Yahweh's gracious saving activity.

Normally, the language of the gospel deals with the good news of salvation that comes to us through the sinless substitute redeemer of the world, Jesus Christ. When St. Augustine said, "Love God and do whatever you want," his declaration assumed a mature understanding of the word *love*. Regarding the evangel, the good news of Jesus, we also need a mature understanding of the word we use for *gospel*. Using an Augustinian wavelength, we might reframe his insight to say, "Faithfully proclaim the gospel—in all articles and live from the gospel—and do whatever you want!" Note well, we live from the gospel; we do not live the gospel. Only Jesus, the embodiment of righteousness, did that!

For Christians who wish to be evangelical to the socks, our view of the gospel must be multi-faceted. Keep in mind that the gospel is like a glorious diamond with all kinds of fabulous facets. It is the good news of how Jesus suffered, died, and bodily rose from the dead. It is the good news of how Jesus perfectly kept the law for us. It is the good news of how God declares the ungodly as godly for Jesus' sake. It is the good news that Jesus is "very God of very God," and that he dwells with us as both God and man through the gift of forgiveness that he prays for us in his role as our great almighty high priest. It is the good news that he grants us his Holy Spirit, that we are saved by grace alone, that he works through us, that he gives us in a spectacularly humble way his true body and blood in the Lord's Supper, and that he has made us his saints. The gospel is the good news of how God the Father, God the Son, and God the Holy Spirit planned our salvation before they created the universe. This is radical grace!

Anything and anyone who attacks these and other facets of the gospel contributes to schism within the body of Christ for such attacks can only strain the body of Christ, cause divisions, rob comfort, take glory away from God, and lead to Tension Deficit Disorder of the theological kind. St. Paul writes, "I appeal to you, brothers, in the name of our Lord Jesus Christ, that all of you agree with one another so that there may be no schisms among you and that you may be perfectly united in mind and thought." (1 Corinthians 1:10)

For the sake of the gospel, Paul will bend over backwards wherever possible, short of compromising the gospel. (1 Corinthians 9:23) His message is that the powerful paradoxical cross and resurrection should be paramount. (1 Corinthians 1:18; 15:1-3) His foundation is the person and work of Christ. (1 Corinthians 3:11) His concern is that the sacraments of baptism and the Lord's Supper should not be reduced to mere rituals but instead seen as gargantuan gospel events (1 Corinthians 10:16; 1

Corinthians 12:13) and that cheap grace should not be the fruit of the gospel, (1 Corinthians 5, 6:1-10) but rather a robust repentance born of justification and baptism marking a Spirit-filled life. (1 Corinthians 6:9-11; 19-20) Gulping the prevalent Epicurean currents of Greek thought, the saints at Corinth were so busy swallowing camels with a type of lawlessness that it made the corruption of the pagans look acceptable by comparison. At the same time, within this seaport city of Corinth there resided gnat-straining legalists who were busily inventing stupid laws that discouraged the right use of the gift of sex within marriage. (1 Corinthians 7)

Paul shows in this letter a wonderful flexibility with weak Christians, (1 Corinthians 8:9-13) but he manifests a holy rigidity when it comes to any rejection of any facet of the gospel. Following a Pauline pattern, the Lutheran church body has not joined in pulpit and altar fellowship with individuals who wish to advance a low octane gospel (Romans 16:17-18) or who short-change any of "the grace of our Lord Jesus." (Romans 16:20) We believe the Holy Spirit's template is this: do not budge an inch when it comes to substitute gospel intrusions. (Galatians 1:6-9) Following the practice of the ancient church for the first 1800 years, we follow closed Communion for the sake of an open gospel. It is something we do because Jesus has commanded us to strive to "observe all things whatsoever he has commanded us." (Matthew 28:16-20)[137] It is the loving thing to do if one is serious about avoiding swallowing camels and straining gnats. It is also very hard to do without straining gnats. While most church bodies today are swallowing camels on this issue by allowing open Communion, as a church body we historically have struggled more with straining gnats. You see, even though closed Communion is a very loving thing to practice according to Jesus and St. Paul; it is very hard to do in a loving way. Nevertheless, let us wrestle with this issue so that we might not suffer from a major case of Tension Deficit Disorder. While I believe we all must sharpen our swords, we must take care not impale one another with haughty, naughty holier-than-thou snideness so indicative of the types of discussions that usually evolve on this tricky matter.

Chapter 17

The Ox is in the Well

Back in the mid-1980s, I had just taken a young woman by the name of Donna through the sixth week of a fourteen-week adult class. The class was designed to prepare Donna to receive the Lord's Supper in a meaningful manner and to teach Donna "all things whatsoever Jesus has commanded." (Matthew 28:16-20) By the grace of God, Donna had abandoned Mormonism, a cult that treats Jesus as less than full God and sufficient Savior. Joy filled Donna as she learned that Jesus was her Savior, her perfect foundation of salvation, the way, the truth, and the life. As a pastor, I was looking forward to Donna coming fully into our communicant fellowship.

Then deep tragedy struck. Donna, just 37, was involved in a car crash and died. A few days later, I conducted her funeral. Through the message of Jesus as the resurrection and life, I consoled her family and friends that Saturday. Donna's husband, a Roman Catholic Christian, was comforted substantially in the midst of this grievous loss knowing that Donna was now with the Lord in heaven.

The next day, the Lord's Day, Donna's husband was one of those in attendance at our Sunday morning worship service. Everyone could see the mountains of grief he still carried on his shoulders despite knowing that Donna was in heaven. Intently, he glued his ears to the Scripture readings, paid close attention to the sermon and listened to the hymns. Knowing the Nicene Creed, he confessed it along with our members confessing Jesus as "very God of very God."

Then came the time to distribute the Lord's Supper. As the first row of saints began to make their way up to the altar, Donna's husband joined the procession. Evidently, he had not read our carefully worded statement in the worship bulletin about guests not in communion fellowship refraining from taking the Lord's Supper. The still rising tears and emotions of grief no doubt hindered that from happening.

Our congregational members who took the catholic New Testament teaching of closed Communion very seriously quickly saw what was unfolding. The singing of the whole congregation tailed off substantially until it was almost a whisper. The saints were no doubt wondering what I was going to do. Ostensibly, at that moment I could sense them praying fervently for me, their pastor, to make a proper decision. A close-knit fellowship, most people knew what had happened in the man's life earlier that same week.

During my seminary training, I learned not to commune non-Lutherans at the local congregational altar. In part, this is because a pastor has no idea if that individual has received instruction on the ABC's of the Lord's Supper. Since a great number of congregations do take people into communion fellowship with little to no instruction, a pastor who is conscientious in terms of care of soul has no way of knowing if this or that guest has been taught at least elementary things about the holiness of God. In addition, because the Lord's Supper is the very body and blood of the all-powerful Son of God in, with, and under the bread and wine, a minister of the cloth cannot dispense it willy-nilly. The Holy Spirit teaches that if a person takes the Lord's Supper in rank unrepentance, it can actually kill them as it did at Corinth. (1 Corinthians 11:29)

Do you see my tension in this situation? As the pastor administering the Lord's Supper, I had a responsibility to follow the Lord's teaching regarding how to administer it and to make sure as far as humanly possible that I was not aiding or abetting anyone in taking the Supper to his or her spiritual and temporal demise. In the Lutheran Church, we believe that both the administrator and the recipient have a mutual responsibility. To say we should leave the whole matter solely up to the person coming to the altar smacks of Tension Deficit Disorder and is a form of swallowing camels. On the other hand, the administrator must take care that he is not going to strain gnats by refusing the Lord's Supper to a Christian who is in dire need.

In some cases of extenuating matters, I believe that a minister may commune a saint from other Christian backgrounds, but closed Communion remains the apostolic tradition. Our seminary students learn that military chaplains have more elbow room and discretionary latitude in these matters than do ministers of community congregations. Likewise, more leniencies fall to pastors serving college campuses. Precisely because these settings necessitate more of a theological triage base of operations rather than the hospital setting of the local congregation, there is a bit more flex. For the rest of us, the general rule remains that we are to practice closed communion. We do this for the sake of the gospel. Paradoxically, only by a good measure of closed communion can one be open to the full gospel. Without a good measure of closed communion we end up with Corinthian confusion. Wide open communion allows different gospels—which are no true gospels—to slip into the church. (Galatians 1:6-7) Ultimately, to make a serious attempt to follow Jesus' instruction to the saints "to observe *all* things whatsoever I have commanded you," (Matthew 28:16-20) we cannot abandoned living in an open-closed communion tension. Moreover, evangelical church bodies have watched churches go to wide open Communion and it isn't long before these church bodies have gone off into the deep end, taking on characteristics of cults rather than remaining as gospel-centered fellowships.

With Donna's husband coming up the aisle towards the altar to receive strength from Christ's true body and blood, (1 Corinthians 10:16) I drew strength from Paul's gospel-centered real-presence understanding of the Lord's Supper. Even so, my theology and practice were tested in those few moments as they have never been tested before. Literally, I could feel the adrenaline surge in my body as I held with trembling hands the cup of blessing. Fervently I cried out to the Lord Jesus in a loud but silent prayer to guide me as to what course of action I should take.

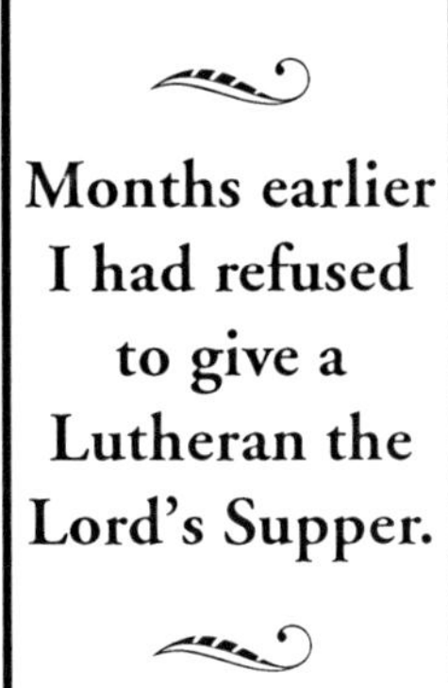
Months earlier I had refused to give a Lutheran the Lord's Supper.

Within my soul I prayed, "Surely he has an idea, O Savior, that you are offering help and your body and blood are present in this holy meal. Yet, O Lord, it is your Supper, not my Supper. You have told us that you want no divisions over the gospel when your people gather. Still, this man is broken with a contrite spirit. He is a bruised reed. I cannot turn him away now lest I add shame, confusion, and rejection to his broken-heartedness."

Months earlier I had refused to give a Lutheran the Lord's Supper. That particular situation involved a man who was a high-ranking lodge member in the area. Proudly he wore the lodge's insignia on his belt buckle. When I tried to explain to him some of the concerns that our church body has against the salvation-by-works philosophy that runs through many lodges, he became angry with me. He started his argument by telling me that the authorities on the lodge whom I quoted were wrong. Getting nowhere, I indicated that we also had a concern over the elements of racism that permeates some lodges.

"I hope you are not planning to invite any darkies to your church," he said to me.

I responded by saying, "First, it is not my church. Second, I plan to invite people from every background and every race because Jesus died for all."

This pseudo Lutheran, like most Lutherans, was not very Lutheran. This man's spirit was the opposite of the spirit embodied by Donna's husband. This lodge member wanted to come to the Lord's Communion

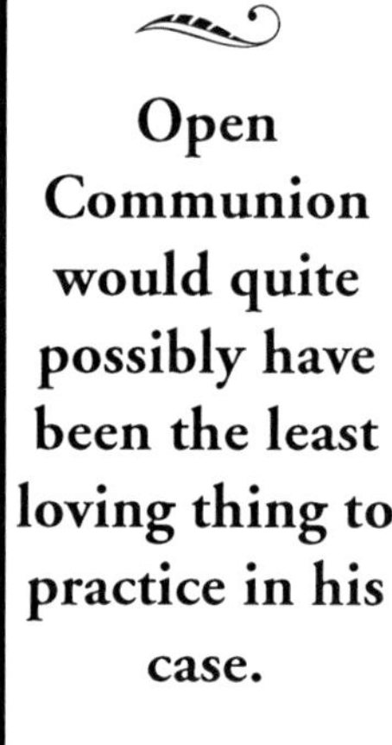

rail with an unrepentant racist attitude. Had I given him the Lord's Supper, I believed that he would have taken this life-giving medicine to judgment. (1 Corinthians 11:29) Open Communion would quite possibly have been the least loving thing to practice in his case.

Nevertheless, Donna's husband came forward a bruised reed, hanging on to life by a mere thread. His faith was like a smoldering wick that I needed to fan back into flame. (Matthew 12:20) I quickly decided that I simply could not turn him away. Concluding that Jesus, whose heel had been bruised on the cross, (Isaiah 53:50) wanted me to bruise Satan's head (Genesis 3:15) by giving Communion to this bruised reed, I communed this non-Lutheran guest, this fellow brother in the one true body of Christ.

Later that same afternoon, I visited Donna's husband at his house to commend him for coming to the Lord's Table. It was at that opportunity that I explained to him more fully the church's historic Communion policy and how we base it upon Christ's dominical word. (Matthew 28:16-20) He gained a better understanding of our closed Communion policy and a door remained ajar for other members of Donna's family to eventually join our church body.

Years ago, former Lutheran Church—Missouri Synod president, Dr. Ralph Bohlmann, explained in a letter to pastors a most helpful way to frame the parameters of our church's paradoxical position on the Communion fellowship issue. It is a position, if I may be so bold as to suggest, which is open and closed at the same time. It helps us to avoid gorging ourselves by swallowing herds of camels and wearing ourselves out by straining vats of gnats.

Since the whole nature of the Lord's Supper is paradoxical, this should not surprise us; that our application of the Lord's Supper would also be paradoxical. After all, the absolute paradox, Jesus Christ, gives us a gift in this meal that we already have—forgiveness—along with bread and wine mixing with his body and blood. While Reformed Christians believe that only bread and wine are present in the Lord's Supper, and while the Christians from Rome believe that only the body and blood of our Lord are present in the Communion elements, Lutherans again take the golden middle path. We believe, teach, and confess that Christ's body and blood are present together with the bread and wine. This we draw from Paul's paradoxical position in Corinthians 10:16 in which he declares, "The cup of blessing which we bless, is it not the communion of the blood of Christ? The bread which we break, is it not the communion of the body of Christ?" In step with this paradoxical disposition of the Lord's Supper, Dr. Bohlmann expresses these beautifully balanced words:

> Two misunderstandings of this position are not uncommon among us, and both deal with the "except" clause. Some virtually ignore this clause and claim that those who make exceptions are practitioners of open Communion. At the other extreme, some pastors and congregations appear to treat exceptions as the rule. The resulting inconsistency between parishes is causing our people a great deal of confusion, and needs to be addressed. I hope you will find ways to do that in this fall's pastoral conferences. In the meantime, please help your people understand that the reason for our synodical positions are Scriptural, and that they are intended to help all of us make a good confession of the faith once delivered to the saints, not only in our individual lives, but also in our corporate actions, including our celebrations of the Lord's Supper.[138]

To avoid Attention Deficit Disorder in Communion practices, the gospel-centered pastor must hold in equal tension Romans 16:17 and Matthew 12:20. If someone is trying to infiltrate ranks with a different gospel, (Galatians 2:4) we dare not budge an inch and are bound, for the sake of the gospel, to practice closed Communion so that we can be open to the gospel. If a Christian is a bruised reed, (Matthew 12:20) or someone like Apollos in the New Testament who is willing to grow and become open to a more full expression of the gospel, (Acts 18:24-26) then one has more flexibility to work towards a closer walk with that person. While the situation does not dictate what to do as it often does using situation ethics, under the Word of God the situation will dictate what passages of the Scripture one should apply. To apply sound passages in an unsound manner merely serves as a pretext for either swallowing camels or straining gnats.

Tension Deficit Disorder can occur in one of two ways when administering the Lord's Supper. We can misuse Romans 16:17 in a wooden way, in cookie-cutter fashion; or we can do, as all too many are doing today, fail to apply it at all. The first results in a brand of legalism. The second paves the way for lawlessness. Neither of these malpractices flows from the gospel.

One of the saints in the congregation where I pastor—a person who is very faithful to our gospel heritage—told me of a saying that her parents sometimes used when she was a girl growing up on the family farm. As far as possible, they family tried on Sunday never to do any hard, physical work. They tried to set aside the Lord's Day for rest of the soul as well as rest of the body. Occasionally, however, when the sun was shining and the crops simply had to be gathered in or risk spoilage, they made an exception to this rule. When those times arose, the lady's mother would say, "The ox is in the well."

Evangelical Christians understand that type of tension, as does our Lord. To theological leaders of his day who were suffering from Tension Deficit Disorder, Jesus said, "If one of you has a son or an ox that falls into a well on the Sabbath day, will you not immediately pull him out?" (Luke 14:5) While situations do not dictate our practice, they do have a bearing as to what passages from Scripture to apply. Context is king. Certain passages become cities of refuge in extraordinary cases. (Joshua 20:1-9) If the intent of a guest is to usher in a different gospel—a sub-grace theology—then closed Communion must be the loving rule lest

Corinthian confusion begins to carve up a congregation. (1 Corinthian 1:10) If belly servers barge up to the Communion rail causing divisions by advancing a different gospel, the Spirit tells us to have nothing to do with them on the plane of fellowship. (Romans 16:17,18) However, if we are dealing with Christians who have merely "fallen in the well," even if they are not fully in communion fellowship, there may be an opportunity for the Lord's Supper to be the hand that pulls these saints up out of the well. In these matters of ministerial discretion, a pastor can tell in a hurry whether such individuals want to embrace the full gospel of the Lord. If they show the kind of openness to catechesis that Apollos expressed upon receiving the full gospel, (Acts 18:24-28) then having lived in the open, yet closed, tension bears a rich harvest. By the way, living in this tension forces the pastor to "pray without ceasing." (1 Thessalonians 5:17)

Chapter 18

Women's Ordination and Tension Deficit Disorder

I have a prayer partner and colleague who is an Episcopalian pastor. Recently, he said to me, "Peter, whatever the Lutheran Church—Missouri Synod does, I pray it will not adopt women's ordination. That change in practice withered our church body. People left in droves. The gospel has been replaced with a radical leftist agenda. We have given up the sacraments. Now we are ordaining unrepentant homosexual pastors."

> **C.S. Lewis warned that should the church ordain women, it would quickly find that it had a whole new religion.**

Years ago, one of the greatest defenders of the gospel, C.S. Lewis, warned that should the church ordain women, it would quickly find that it had a whole new religion.[139] After a generation spent watching mainline church bodies ordain women, I believe we have seen the truth of that prediction by C.S. Lewis. Not content simply to ordain women, these church bodies are clamoring to swallow new camels by ordaining lesbians and homosexuals. Along with this worldview, these church bodies have bought hook, line, and sinker into the historical critical view of Biblical interpretation.

The historical critical (sometimes abbreviated as HC) method of Biblical interpretation, with its anti-miraculous bias, is the queen that rules the theological formulation of the vast majority of seminaries in many mainstream denominations. This is tragic on several fronts. I have friends who attended such seminaries tell me they had virtually no faith at all upon graduation. One member of the clergy said that he had to buy a book on miracles in order to restore his own faith in Jesus.

Not only does the historical critical method undermine confidence in God's Word, but it also works with the assumption that we must find God by determining for ourselves which texts of Scripture to uphold or to let fall. This is gnat straining. It leads to legalism. It makes God look like a doofus hipster when it comes to the whole matter of the inspiration of Scripture. The gospel teaches that God finds us through the text with his Word of forgiveness in Christ. At the base of the historical critical method is the pagan ethos of salvation by works.

In addition, the historical critical method ends up being an eclectic dialectic where you pick and chose what fits your particular theological system. It invariably ends up in severe Tension Deficit Disorder. The Bible tells us that it is the Holy Spirit that quickens, converts, and brings one to faith in Jesus via the gospel. (1 Corinthians 12:3; 2 Thessalonians 2:14) Consequently, in matters of salvation, the historical critical method replaces the gospel with a new law; man must find God. The historical critical method leads to relativistic formulations in the field of ethics thus weakening the law-gospel dialectic, and it shows little sense of paradox in virtually every key doctrine of the Bible from inspiration to the nature of the Lord's Supper and to the person of Christ.

A stunning article on the subject of women's ordination appeared in the spring 2004 issue of *Lutheran Forum*. It came from the keyboard of a vicar of the Evangelical Lutheran Church of America—a church body that embraces the ordination of women. The article, *"How My Mind Has Changed,"* revealed how the movement to ordain women into the office of the holy ministry brought with it all kinds of unintended consequences. Wrote Vicar Smith:

> Feminist women clergy and their male supporters have carried this revision, through our seminaries, which are all too beholden to the modern religious academy, into the parish life of the church. This movement is manifest in the monstrosities of the so-called inclusive language and of sexual relations outside of marriage. This manifestation is only the tip of the iceberg: below the surface is a rejection of the God of Scripture in favor of the chthonic deities that the Bible was written to oppose. Now human religion has come to replace divine Biblical revelation.[140]

From a purely practical point of view, the track record toward women's ordination invariably takes a header toward ecclesiastical nihilism. History is painfully clear on this matter. Without exception, every church body that has gone down the road of women's ordination slowly begins the path to forfeiting their theological heritage. Theological language within these church bodies starts taking on the form of fog. The clear good news of free forgiveness, life, and salvation through Jesus Christ as the only Savior of sinners is elbowed out of the center replaced by worldly views. Totalitarian tendencies as well as libertine leanings creep in incrementally. Over time everything is a theological blur. Power politics—what we must do—take precedent over serious discussions about the nature of the good news of Jesus—our real power. (Romans 1:16)

What is so deadly about this descent toward nihilism is that the power politics church bodies with their narrow human law-driven methods become so tolerant they become intolerant to the ABC's of the Christian faith. Let me cite a prime example of this. Recently elected Episcopal Bishop Katherine Schori declared in the summer of 2006, "Homosexuality is not a sin."[141] Her denomination in the same year refused to affirm the words of Jesus in John 14:6 and the need by all for the message of the cross. Tragically, the very thing necessary to keep one from slipping into extremes, the message of the cross, could not muster enough support for an "Amen" from this once very Calvary-centered, Jesus-centered, gospel-centered church body.

One of the biggest problems within the movement to ordain women is the failure to ask the Jesus question: What has the Lord Jesus ordained in regard to this matter? In raising this question a gospel-centered interpreter sees the issue of ordination into the office of the Holy Ministry as above all a Jesus thing, not a human thing. Whereas a gospel-centered approach sees the matter of ordination in dual polarities, advocates of women's ordination see only half the equation. For them, qualified functional competence of candidates apt to teach is the sole measuring stick. Yet, the Holy Spirit moves panoplied readers of the Bible to examine another crucial component to this issue. Again, we can frame it in the question: "What has Jesus ordained?"

Through his prime-time interpreter St. Paul, Jesus makes very clear how he wants his gospel distributed in the arena of public worship. Paul, using the totality of the Hebrew Scriptures as his norm, argues that pastors are to be called men apt to teach. (1 Corinthians 14:21, 34, 1 Timothy 3:1-7) Like the message of the cross this odd arrangement is a sheer scandal to all humanistic manifestos. Yet whether the message of salvation itself or how this message is to be publicly distributed, it is not for us to veto by a pick-and-choose TDD hermeneutic. Paul the brilliant Hebrew student of the celebrated Jewish teacher Gamaliel rooted the office of the holy ministry in the male priesthood arrangements that God first set forth—"even as the Law and Gospel of the Torah says." (1 Corinthians 14:21, 34, *Free Translation*)

"What has Jesus ordained?" Ask St. Paul. He will tell you to study the template of the Hebrew Bible. "What has Jesus ordained?" Study Jesus' Hebrew Bible! To really get at the issue of women's ordination in a true Messianic fashion, we need to pay closer attention to the gospel distribution arrangements in both the Old and New Testament.

When the manner of Jesus' gospel work gives way to pure utilitarianism, this ends up not being very practical. Why? The gospel—God's power—ends up getting covered by the fungus of raw functionalism. Functionalism trumps Jesus' arrangement and invariably the gospel—what God graciously does, plays third fiddle to how humans must function in setting up their version of the kingdom of God.

How does this play out? Several ways. Back in the 1990s, I spent considerable time as a hobby reading sermons by women who had been ordained. The common note of their homilies was law, law, and more law. Rarely could you find any message of the good news of full forgiveness, free salvation, and the death of Jesus on the cross. Little did I hear about how Jesus comes to us through his means of grace. Seldom did you read about the fabulous facets of the gospel. This should not surprise anyone. If the basis for a woman becoming a pastor—*pastor* is a masculine word in the New Testament—was a one-sided functional approach, then a lopsided emphasis on doing would be natural and normative.

Similarly, for more than twelve years I have been part of a ministerial alliance in which three of the represented churches have had four clergywomen during these years. All of these women are fine Christians, competent servants of Christ in terms of helping people with a host of needs. I have high regard for each of them. I have prayed for all of them. I have found each of them to be *tremendous* blessings to our community. However, the one thing needful above all things in pastoral ministry is to get the good news of Jesus out so that the Holy Spirit might do his most important work. In twelve years, I have yet to see any of these women write an article for our local newspaper through our Ministerial Alliance that contains the explicit gospel. Likewise, I have yet to hear from any of them a clear proclamation of the message of the cross. Rather, the dominant note, if not in some cases the exclusive note, is what God wants us to do instead of what Yahweh has done through his wonderful Son. Forgiveness of sins through the bringer of salvation is not at the core of their collected messages. At best, this core tenet of the Bible is peripheral in their proclamation and this, I believe, leads these women to a theology where the law is the dominant note.

The very fact that the ordination of women is a Johnny-come-lately seismic shift in the practice of the church certainly draws major question marks from church historians. Usually we associate such shifts with Johnny-come-lately cults such as the Jehovah's Witnesses, the Mormons, and the Moonies. Common to these cults as well as the movement of the ordination of women is a thoroughly law-centered, law-driven, works-righteous emphasis. So often, radical liberal theology joins hands with the cults thus minimizing the atonement of Jesus Christ (1 John 2:2) as the source of regenerating power.

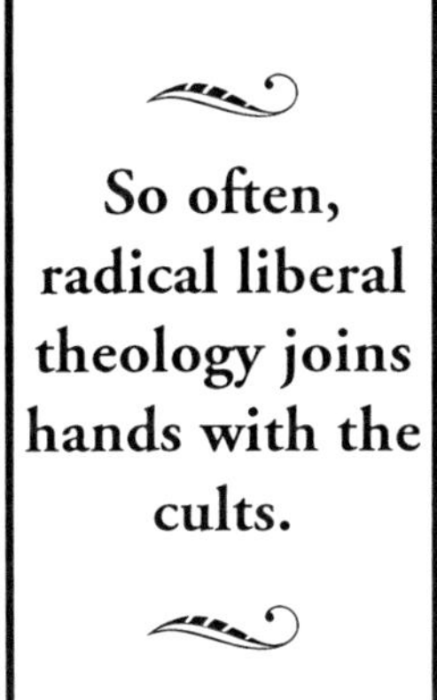

Good church historians will also tell us that neither in the Old Testament nor in the New Testament do we have anything remotely close to women being pastors. The preferred office of public ministry for women is the office of a deaconess, a noble office in the line of Phoebe. (Romans 16:1) I once asked one of our ladies what she would think if I expressed a desire to be a deaconess.

Gertie just laughed as and said, "Pastor, you just would not look good in a dress."

Behind the humor of this 92-year-old saint's response was the sense that God has set up certain offices for men and certain offices for women, that we should embrace his gracious arrangements, and that we should not pick from forbidden fruit.

Students of the Bible rightly argue that there were women prophetesses in the Bible. Hulda and Philip's daughters were among them. In the Old Testament, Deborah was a judge. Priscilla was a missionary and bringer of good news. What is noticeably missing is any indication that the Messianic women of antiquity were priests or pastors; the two offices that foreshadow and fulfill one another. Added to this, if any woman would have ever been more than qualified to be a pastor by divine grace it would have been Mary, the mother of God. Luke, in Acts, gives not the slightest indication of anything that would have leaned toward the ordination or women.

The Lord of the church has set up a theological win/win regarding this whole matter. It is simple without being simplistic. Hold high the office of the holy ministry for men and hold high the office of deaconess for women. That arrangement is in step with the substantial Old and New Testament thrusts on this issue and it serves the effort to keep the gospel at the center of the church's proclamation.

Proponents of women's ordination suffer major Tension Deficit Disorder when they stop their ears to Paul's words:

> "For God is not the author of confusion, but of peace, as in all the congregations of the saints, let your women keep silence in the churches: for it is not permitted unto them to speak; but they are commanded to be under obedience, as also saith the law."
>
> (1 Corinthians 14:34)

If this verse means anything, at a bare minimum it must mean that women are not publicly to proclaim the word of God in a worship service. That is the context. It is very specific about how Jesus wants the gospel administered in divine worship services. It is universal to all the congregations of the holy ones. At the same time, it holds open almost endless possibilities for women to serve the Savior within the church as directors of Christian education, missionaries, Christian day school teachers, deaconesses, music directors, and more.

Almost every year, about three-quarters of the way through the confirmation classes of our seventh and eighth grade students, some thoughtful young woman will ask me the perennial spring question. "Pastor, is it permissible for a woman to be a pastor?"

"According to the Holy Spirit who gives us a sure word in Scripture, the answer is no," I will then answer.

"Why?" she will invariably continue with the question.

"Because women are too smart," I will respond with a smile.

Stunned, the young woman will not know what to say. She likes the compliment but appears to feel straitjacketed by paradox in a double bind.

At that point, I invariably will go on with the topic at hand. After another two minutes or so, the same young woman will usually ask me to explain my previous response more fully.

I will then tell her that if it were simply a matter of ability and function, then without a doubt women could be pastors. Jesus though, has not set up his office for pastors this way. For whatever deep reasons, our Lord has set forth this scandal of particularity, this article of faith and love, for the well-being of his bride, the church. As indicated earlier, church bodies that have rejected this arrangement by Jesus of the public distribution of the means of grace have met with disaster, sacrificed facets of the gospel, and morphed into chaos or libertine immorality. Through his apostle to the Gentiles, St. Paul, Jesus made clear how he wants his gospel to go forth, especially in the realm of corporate worship. (John 17:20; 1 Corinthians 14: 34–40)[142]

How else does Tension Deficit Disorder crop up in the matter of the ordination of women? It emanates when people fail to understand the paradoxical nature of the dance within the Holy Trinity. Specifically, TDD results from a failure to grasp the relationship of Jesus and the Father in terms of time and eternity. The gospel makes clear that Jesus and God are equal. (John 10:30; John 20:28; Colossians 2:9) Despite being equal to the Father, at the end of history Jesus will subject himself under the authority of the Father. (1 Corinthians 15:24-28) The paradox is that Jesus, although equal, will submit himself to the authority of the Father in a beautiful transaction of giving and receiving. Equal to God, Jesus will rank himself under the Father. Truly, the tension between equality and authority presents a deep mystery of the faith and presents the paradigm or model for how men and women are to interact in ministry.

Within the body of Christ, men and women are also on equal footing through the gospel miracle of holy baptism. (Galatians 3:26-29) Women's ordination proponents suffer Tension Deficit Disorder when they enlist this reality to erase lines of authority—also a gift—that God has set up in Christ's church through the office of the holy ministry. Here's the deal: we should not use God's gift of equality to eliminate God's gift of authority.

Think about it. When Paul writes that women, in relationship to the pastor's office, (1Timothy 2:1-12) are not "to usurp authority" over men, he is harkening back to the relationship of the Father to the Son. In Christ, women are to celebrate through baptism their equal footing with men! This was radical New Testament Equal Rights Amendment talk thanks to St. Paul (Galatians 3:26-29) as well as the very stuff that would take down slavery in the ancient world. Women are to accept their Christ-like role of submission in light of the *parousia* when Jesus will submit himself to the Father for all eternity. (1 Corinthians 15:24-28) Meanwhile, men are to submit to the gospel order to love women with the slave-like love of Christ. (Ephesians 5:25, Philippians 2:4-11) Where this breaks down, you get feminism or fundamentalism, a lawless spirit or a legalist spirit, swallowing camels or straining gnats. Tragically, wherever you find the omission of double submission, you find major Tension Deficit Disorder as well as general disorder.

Sadly, it is the male leadership within the church and the office of the holy ministry that is a big culprit here. For decades, gospel-deficient seminary professors intoxicated by the "you-find-god teachings of the world" and "the quest for empowerment" movements have peddled lopsided, shortsighted views regarding the office of the holy ministry. Made tipsy by the salvation-by-works liquors of the historical critical method, the Spirit's crisp coherent witness from Jesus, Paul, and the apostles has given way to the zigzag course of a drunken peasant. The texts of Scripture for the sake of the gospel are not allowed to speak for themselves and are not held in tension. Likewise, men have been all too happy to dump more and more work of the church on women as the men all head for the hills, the fishing holes, the bar rooms, and other venues. Unless church bodies can return to a full paradoxical gospel, one can expect the mainline church bodies to become more matriarchal, more legalistic, and more lawless. Lack of theological balance will be the trumpet sound, shrill and uncertain. Swallowing camels and straining gnats will be the heritage of a Christendom that lacks the leavening power of the gospel unto salvation.

Chapter 19

CONCLUSION

Wisdom literature of the Bible beckons us to be friendly contrarians. (Proverbs 16:7) When we see the crowd going one direction, it usually is a good idea to go the opposite way. (1 Corinthians 10:8; Genesis 6:18) Most people, however, are going the wrong way. (Matthew 7:13-14) Says Solomon, "There is a way which seemeth right unto a man, but the end thereof are the ways of destruction." (Proverbs 14:12) Wisdom literature also tells us that the man and the woman of God will try to avoid the extremes of legalism and lawlessness. (Ecclesiastes 7:18) Since all religions, with the exception of Christianity, are by nature legalistic to the core, only Christianity holds hope for mankind to avoid the way of destruction. Only Christianity lets God be God through his paradoxical means of grace at work through his paradoxical people.

Through these past chapters, I have sought to demonstrate the paradoxical nature of Christianity in general and the gospel in particular. It begins with God's paradoxical good news that God, for the sake of Jesus, declares the ungodly as godly. (Romans 4:5) It centers upon the absolute paradox, Jesus Christ. (John 1:1-14) It focuses upon how God comes to us in time and space. In the fullness of time, he takes an instrument of death—the cross—and turns it into an instrument of life.

Christianity also celebrates the paradoxical nature of how God comes to us through the externals of Word and sacrament and the body of Christ so that we might grasp the internals of faith, hope, and love. (Titus 3:5; Matthew 26:28; John 20:21-23) We see so that we believe is the way of this good news revelation.

Do we have today a special opening to advance this good news? John Leo wrote about "the good news generation" in the November 3, 2003, issue of *U.S. News & World Report.* Born before 1946 and part of a four-generation family, John Leo says the watchwords of his generation were *duty*, *tradition*, and *loyalty*. His spouse, a baby boomer, came from a generation often noted for its individuality, tolerance, and self-absorption.

Leo's first two daughters, known as part of Generation X that is shortened to Gen X-ers, come from a subgroup of the populace known for its "diversity, savvy, and pragmatism." His youngest daughter, born between 1977 and 1994, is part of the millennial generation, also known as Generation Y or the echo boomers. In one family, then, there is a builder, a boomer, a buster, and a bridger, to use the language that is in vogue today.

Thoughtful people know that these divisions are loaded with exceptions. Many more templates affect personality in addition to the year in which one is born. However, there are patterns here that the church should note, not ignore. Throughout the Bible, one senses a shifting of patterns and priorities from one generation to the next. When we can use this information in service of the gospel, it is good stewardship.

Which traits of the 78 million millennials might be significant? Being concerned about the family, wanting to be authentic, and being oriented toward the paradoxical are all in step with aspects of Christian revelation. All three give us some common ground on which to apply Biblical truths. In other words, people today are so weary of so many extremes that they may be doubly open to the paradoxical heritage of the gospel. This new generation has seen the suicidal path of people who swallow camels (libertines) and has witnessed the suffocating paths of those straining gnats (legalists). As a result, the balanced path that Jesus brings, takes, and offers through the gospel may have particular appeal. For the sake of the gospel, we must seize this potential redemptive moment before it comes and we miss it. (Galatians 6:10)

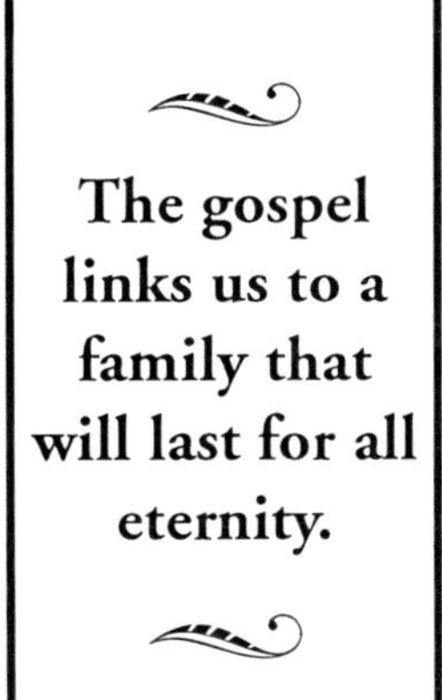

When a person studies these generations and their patterns, one should also see how the gospel touches all the bases. Really, "the hopes and fears of all the years" are met and addressed in the person and work of Jesus. Every one of the needs of each of these generations can be more than met through the rich, fabulous facets of the gospel. Builders need a sense of good tradition. The gospel is a tradition that goes all the way back to the garden of Eden. (Genesis 3:15). It actually reaches back before time! (Ephesians 1:3-5) Boomers long to belong. I know because I am one with this generation. The gospel links us to a family that will last for all eternity in the new heaven and new earth. Busters are willing to work for a good cause—what better cause than the cause of the gospel—a message that has brought more good to the world in terms of compassion, a coherent view of the universe, and universal grace. Finally, the bridger pines for a longer life span and yearns for paradoxes; the gospel grants immortality to mortals and is, by far and away, the post paradoxical message on the face of the earth!

A paradoxical gospel-centered vision is vital for another reason in addition to its timeliness. Right now in our church body as well as in most church bodies, the trust level among members is low. Even in the context of a fallen world, one would like to see more trust among the saints. Here we must ask an important question. What is the essence of good trust? How is it actually engendered in a church, in a government, or in a marriage? It does not come from people saying, "Trust me, trust me, and please trust me." That is a law move, not a gospel move.

The curb and cure for suspicion is born of a common commitment to the full gospel of our Lord Jesus Christ. Salutary trust comes and grows from a mature faith in the Absolute Paradox. The gospel not only fights extremes by its very nature, but it is the great glue for a wholesome trust that is needed when walking together and working together within the body of Christ. Beautiful bonds are born when common commitment to the person and work of Jesus are established and grow. Nevertheless, where legalism replaces the gospel and where lawlessness serves as a 666 version of the gospel, trust erodes, church bodies fracture, homes melt down, and cultures are carried away by extremes.

In the New Testament, the Greek word *pistis* is used for the English words of *faith*, *trust*, and *believe*. *Pistis* is the root word for our English word *epistemology*. When St. Paul uses this word in Romans 10:17, he gives a significant clue to understand how God-pleasing trust is born. He writes, "Trust comes from hearing the message and the message is heard through the paradoxical word of Christ." (*Free Translation*)

Mark where this passage leads us. The message of the suffering, death, and resurrection of Jesus, along with the many other fascinating gospel facets, is the key for the trust level to grow in society as well as in the church. Where faith comes forth, love appears. Where love appears, goodwill arises. Where goodwill arises, people can walk together in harmony. In the end, this love, trust, and goodwill must find its foundation in the person, work, and teachings of the absolute paradox. To the degree that the church can navigate this kind of course, it can prepare people to contend with the seduction of extremes.

When the good news about Jesus takes root in a person's life through the forgiveness that Jesus brings, a person becomes more dependable, more trustworthy, more honest, and more true to his word. When this good news—in the fullness of its fabulous facets—becomes the good ground on which individuals stand, common ground develops. This has a wonderful way of lowering suspicions and getting all of us on the same theological page. As it is now, within church bodies there are terrible temptations to fight out differences through bylaws, backroom ecclesiastical politics, caricatures, and lawsuits rather than going to our concord power source: the full, mighty and meaty gospel of the Lord Jesus.

There is a paradoxical catch, however. Where trust in Jesus arises through the church, the message of the cross, Christian love, and the means of Word and Sacrament, Christians become more suspicious in one realm and yet more trusting in another. We become more suspicious toward the Tension Deficit Disorder doctrines of the world (1 John 4:1; Colossians 2:8) even as the gospel produces good works in us that silence suspicion mongers. (1 Peter 3:16) This cross-borne attitude of being simultaneously suspicious when it comes to evil things and reducing unhealthy suspicion by doing God-pleasing things curbs naiveté even as it cultivates good will. The gift of faith in Christ in this manner creates the biblical balance needed to walk wisely in our gullible yet cynical world.

Families that live from the paradoxical gospel of our Lord Jesus Christ also profit substantially. The Spirit helps a gospel-centered family so that validation, confirmation, and affirmation in Christ are the dominant notes rather than the accusatory fingers of the law. Where the good news of Christ's love—free forgiveness, robust use of the gift of repentance, and joy—dominates the landscape of a home, then Tension Deficit Disorder will not allow a family to become too authoritarian or too permissive. Where the paradoxical gospel dwells in family members richly, there will be a holy conjunction of God's life-enhancing law and life-giving Spirit. (Romans 13:10; Galatians 5:22-23)

Paramount to the church doing vigorous mission work is to have a paradoxical gospel to inspire its people to witness as well as to give generously for missions. Where the gospel sinks into all the compartments of life, there is a strong impetus for Christians to be at the same time frugal and generous. They want to be frugal as possible to put every dime, dollar, and ducat that Jesus gives towards the extension of Christ's Kingdom. At the same time, they are generous in all areas of life even as they save for the future. They know that good works are important; ironically, so that people learn that good works do not save us Christians.

Jesus expressed the paradox of giving in this manner, "Give, and it shall be given unto you; good measure, pressed down, and shaken together, and running over." (Luke 6:38) However, where there are theological forms of deficit disorders, one can only expect financial deficits due to breakdowns on all fronts. Whether it is the diversion of large sums of money within the church to conduct ecclesiastical campaigns for electing the right person or prince to lead us through the wilderness, or whether it is keeping so much of the Lord's money to invest in stuff that has no enduring power, Tension Deficit Disorder causes breakdown in this realm as well.

Closely related to this is another matter; the urgency with which we exercise the gift of prayer for wisdom to guard against exaggerated activity as well as a growing inaction so that we can determine the Mary/Martha balance in life. Only then will we more clearly see Jesus, regain our balance in priorities, and be equipped to be able to resist enslavement to the extremes of this age. Our age is one in which we can easily find ourselves overextended and under-befriended. When that happens we lapse into a spiritual-physical funk as did Elijah after his battle with the salvation-by-works prophets of Baal. Overextended and under-befriended, Elijah took an extremely pessimistic view on life. Only when the absolute paradox, the angel of the Lord, Jesus the Christ, made a special guest appearance to him did Elijah rebound. (1 Kings 19:7) Through physical rest, good food, an excellent aerobics walking program, paradoxical thinking, and coming back into fellowship with other believers of the remnant, Elijah did eventually bounce back into a paradoxical "yet, not yet" mindset. (1 Kings 19)

The Tension Deficit Disorder syndrome looms large not only in the Missouri Synod, but throughout evangelicalism. Cambridge scholar Os Guinness argues that anti-intellectualism has become the scandal of evangelicalism. In his book "*Fit Bodies, Fat Minds*," he documents how within evangelicalism there is a strong tendency for Christians to be lightweights intellectually. Of course, in one sense this is nothing new. In his day, Bertrand Russell said, "Most Christians would rather die than think—in fact they do."[143] What Russell witnessed in his day to draw this conclusion was not true Christianity being played out. Jesus, the master teacher, tells us that we are to love the Lord with all our heart, mind, body, and soul. (Mark 12:30) We are to be rational without being rationalistic.

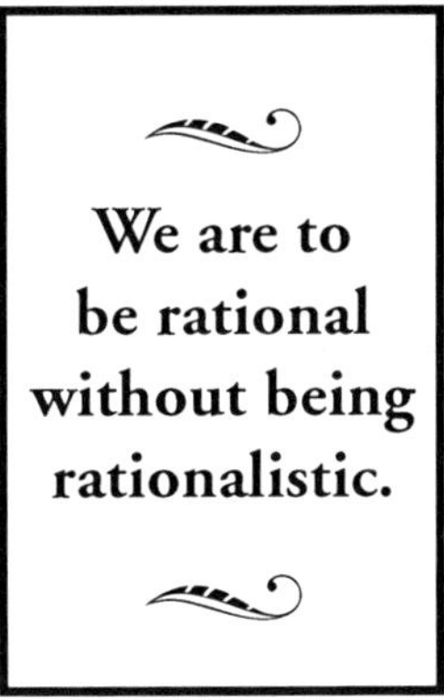

Paradox in service of the gospel challenges us to love the Lord with our entire mind, making careful distinctions, and paying close attention to context as we search the nooks and crannies of the Scriptures. (John 5:39) "Think! Think! Think!" Jesus says to his disciples. (Mark 8:15-21) From his parables to his paradoxical Sermon on the Mount to his passion on the paradoxical death/life tree, Jesus is enjoining his disciples to think seriously. He does not want us to set up a false antagonism between heart and head. A wholesome piety that avoids legalistic pietism and advocates rigorous thinking with a heart of humility adorn well the gospel. Blaise Pascal, a savant as brilliant as any individual this past millennium, once scribbled this note, "pious scholars—very rare."[144] In service of the gospel, paradox seeks to avoid both the extremes of anti-intellectualism as well as lack of piety.

If I had time, I would love to write a book titled, "All the Einsteins of the Bible." From Moses to Joseph to Ezra to David to Solomon to Daniel to Mary to Matthew to Luke to John to Peter and Paul, we see how God used a long list of saints that sought to love him with their minds as well as their hearts and souls. From Mary's paradoxical *Magnificat* to John's stunning Greek structure in Revelation, from the profound treatment of matters of justice and righteousness by Moses to the prophet Amos' high rhetoric and uncanny defense of the underdog, one sees that serious thinking in service of the gospel is the on-going norm. Then you have St. Paul, an Einstein-like cosmological thinker,

(Colossians 1:15-20; 2:9) and his wunderkind friend Luke, the physician, who team up as a dynamic duo to tell the story of Jesus in a fabulous fashion. Above all, you have Jesus loving God the Father with all his mind, heart, soul, and strength.

As a second related aside, the American Film Institute came out with the top 100 songs from U.S. films. Two of the top three were paradoxical in music and movement. Number three was "*Singing in the Rain*" with its grand nevertheless of faith flowing through the veins of that hit. The number one pick was *"Over the Rainbow"* which had a beautiful tune that was a paradoxical mixture of haunting hope. You will recall that one of the great themes through the characters of Frank Baum's book "The Wonderful Wizard of Oz" was the need for the Scarecrow, Tin Woodsman and the Lion to get a heart, a brain, and courage. Paradox in service of the gospel sees how the gospel provides all three attributes through the love of the Absolute Paradox who perfectly manifested all three characteristics.[146]

In our day of extremes, we witness one drunken ideology after another rising from hell and offering us heaven. Invariably, all of them suffer from Tension Deficit Disorder playing out in the form of swallowing camels or straining gnats. The only way to avoid the seduction of extremes is to take a paradoxical path in life. Adolph Köberle describes that path:

> To keep one's balance on a narrow mountain path or on a tight rope is apparently a static act; in fact, it is possible only as a ceaseless progress. So the unsolved paradox of the grace of forgiveness and renewal, the effort to attain a unity of faith and action immediately reminds us that we have not yet come home, that we are still on our way, as "pilgrims and strangers." ... We find a true Christian eschatology only where the decree of justification and sanctification, possessing and not possessing, perfection and imperfection, are ever experienced together. Whoever tries to speak without paradoxes and would consider each one of these realms alone, who tries to find a solution of the paradox now,

> betrays either Good Friday or Easter and fails to understand our present status between Pentecost and the Parousia, in which it is equally sin and disobedience against God if we do not "grow in grace" or if we seek to anticipate the glory of the final perfection.[147]

We see here how the paradoxical mindset runs for the sake of the gospel. We assert one truth and then we must quickly set forth the opposite yet balancing truth. Paradox works the two hands of faith—the left hand as well as the right hand—simultaneously. Unless we do this we will spin our theological wheels in turmoil, speak with half a tongue, and fall either into the ditch of legalism or lawlessness, straining gnats or swallowing camels as we do. Mary C. Morrison poetically sums up the dance of paradox:

> Paradox loves and moves in this realm: it is the art of balancing opposites in such a way that they do not cancel each other but shoot sparks of light across their polarity. It looks at our desperate either/ors and tells us they are really both/ands—that life is larger than any of our concepts and can, if we let it, embrace our contradictions.[148]

As a Christian who strives to be gospel-centered, I am more comfortable with the wording in the last line as "seeming" contradictions. Flat contradictions take us into the world of oxymoron. Paradox in service of the gospel holds together two opposite truths lest we lapse into legalism or lunge into lawlessness. The heart of the Scriptures, the soul of the gospel, and the very nature of God are paradoxical to the core. This has been the thesis of this book. If this modest effort helps you avoid a measure of swallowing camels and straining gnats, "God be praised!" If this book helps you to see the beautiful balance in Scripture that is pulled together by the person and work of Jesus, "God be praised!"

If it leads you to exclaim, "What a wonderful Savior we have in Jesus Christ!" God be praised!

While swallowing camels and straining gnats may be the order of the day, we do not have to follow this path toward extremism. By God's grace, if evangelical Christianity can find its way back to its royal roots of a gospel-centered paradoxical theology, then there is huge hope. A genuine reformation that would bless this nation and this world could yet occur before the glorious reappearing of our ever-present Lord. (2 Timothy 4:8) If not, a badly wounded, self-inflicting, overly argumentative Tension Deficit Disorder sub-gospel brand of Christianity will be bequeathed to our children, and to our children's children. Such an anemic gospel will provide little help for the saints to contend with the fierce forces of extremism that the devil will marshal in these last days. Yet, even as I write these things, I can give no better advice than to say that we should live as though Jesus died the day before yesterday, rose yesterday, and is coming today.

ENDNOTES

1. Bill O'Reilly, *The No Spin Zone*, (New York: Broadway Books, 2001), pp. 9-16. Similarly, it is a well-known fact in the Middle East that radical Muslim men often have no scruples when it comes to taking a small child as one's wife or part of a harem.
2. George Barna, *Think Like Jesus,* (Nashville: Integrity Publishers, 2003), p.24.
3. Michael Novak, *On Two Wings*, (San Francisco: Encounter Books, 2002), p.7. Novak's point is not an exaggeration. The founders and framers of our government were tethered to the Torah and steeped in the Scriptures and thus rooted in a Biblical realism. Note the flavor of the following quotes which are anything but an anomaly. George Washington once declared, "It is impossible to rightly govern the world without God and the Bible." Abraham Lincoln similarly stated, "I believe the Bible is the best gift God ever communicated." Daniel Webster stated it stronger yet, "If we abide by the principles taught in the Bible, our country will go prospering." [All three quotes are from *Notable Quotables, pp. xii & xiii,* preface to the *New Evangelical Translation,* (Cleveland: Net Publishing, 1988). For full documentation of how freely and

frequently the founding fathers drew from the Bible see not only Novak's book but also see David Barton's *Original Intent*, (Aledo, Texas: WallBuilders, 2005). In our post modern age, many people want the fruits of freedom without the roots of freedom. This is a dangerous disconnect. To aid and abet this disconnection there has been a strenuous effort to rewrite history. Thus, major revisionist efforts have been made to minimize the crucial role of the Hebrew Scriptures and the New Testament Scriptures in providing prime time ideological influence and inspiration to the birth of our nation. Ultimately, the Bible is so beautifully balanced on church and state matters if one can avoid the eclectic dialectic. The inspiration of Christ's love and the insights of the Scriptures were two elements in the water of early Americans and a critical mass of our nation's founders and populace drank heartily these living waters. One crucial example among many will show the brilliant Biblical balance. Jesus carefully taught a doctrine of two kingdoms (Matthew 22:21). This doctrine as delineated by Jesus is a cure for the extreme of theocracy, while his Sermon on the Mount (Matthew 5:13-16 is a cure for the opposite of theocracy: complete separation of church and state. Again Solomon, "The man who fears God will avoid all extremes" (Ecclesiastes 7:16).

4. Brennan Manning, *The Ragamuffin Gospel* (Sisters, Oregon: Multnomah Publishers, 1990), pp. 20-21.
5. Unless otherwise marked, Scripture quotations are from the King James Version of the Bible. There will be some personal translations from the Hebrew and Greek to bring out the force of the original.
6. Gospel restrictionism is a term I have coined to get at the opposite error of gospel reductionism since temptations come in opposites. We have the lard of one and the cholesterol of the other to keep out of our theological arteries. It may seem strange to some that I have defined "gospel reductionism" as a reduced gospel, but that is what it ends up becoming in reality. Originally, many people

who used the term "gospel reductionism" sought to use it so that the good news of forgiveness of sins that the Lord Jesus brings was the paramount piece of Christian proclamation. Amen. Unfortunately, when an extremely narrow view of the gospel became the sole norm for theology at the expense of the exile of the law, an unintended consequence occurred. When the law of God was diminished—which serves in part, as "a mirror bright to bring the inbred sin to light," (Romans 3:20) the good news of free and full forgiveness also took a hit. The two must be properly held in tension lest the law be wrongly used and the gospel be reduced to some bland good news devoid of its many powerful gospel facets. A theologian friend of mine summed up the mindset of most gospel reductionists today, "As long as I believe in Jesus, I am not going to sweat the details." Major TDD attitude! Jesus wants to be more than a messianic mantra. The New Testament book of Colossians gives us a clear picture of the quantitative and qualitative view of Jesus the Holy Spirit wants us to embrace while Galatians presents a dynamic picture of his work. It's all about Jesus. Anything that detracts from His person and work will lead toward some kind of seduction of extremes.

7. What tragically happens between parties where excess becomes an abscess is the dialogue of the deaf. People talk past one another or cease to talk to one another. As a result, the chasm of misunderstanding grows.
8. Paul Maier, *Jesus First*, (Issue 49, November 2005), p. 3.
9. Elton Trueblood, *The Philosophy of Reason*, (New York: Harpers Brothers, 1957), p. 125. The word paradox is often used by people today in a variety of ways—some lethal. For example, Dr. John Warwick Montgomery alerts us how in much of modern theology, "paradox inevitably associates with the Neo-Orthodox, Barthian notion that truth is never univocal and human language cannot therefore present it in an unqualified, apodictic manner. It follows that the Bible cannot be, in itself, the Word of God: It

can only point beyond itself to the transcendent Word of God. This understanding of paradox is therefore utterly deadly to any classical attempt to defend the Incarnation—and, indeed, the trustworthiness or perspicuity of Scripture." [From personal correspondence May 30, 2006]. The servant use of paradox that holds together two truthful Biblical propositions in sharp tension will reveal the beautiful balance and consistent coherence that runs throughout the whole of Scripture. Unlike Hegel who used paradox to dissolve truth, Luther, Pascal, Lewis, Augustine, and Köberle used this servant tool to hold together God's ferocious revealing and concealing opposites. From Genesis to Revelation the Holy Spirit's dynamic dual assertions of Scripture clearly and cleanly unceasingly swerve between legalism and lawlessness. Christianity is the only religion that averts the seduction of both extremes.

10. Some saints may object to my calling Saul a terrorist. They will argue that he had the Jewish law on his side to go and do what he did. Having lawless law on one's side does not diminish the fact that in terms of real life experience St. Paul behaved like a terrorist. I don't want to strain gnats on this terminology, but to emphasize how the radical love of Jesus is the one thing alone that can really change terrorists.

11. This term *Tension Deficit Disorder* came about in a Bible study with the Jefferson City and Columbia circuit pastors of the Lutheran Church—Missouri Synod sometime in the year 2003. Pastor Tony Alter, Pastor Gerald Scheperle, myself, and others, were bantering back and forth words and this combination arose. It summarizes well a malady church bodies today are facing. My point here is that the whole two circuits of this fine group of evangelical pastors deserves credit for this handy phrase. One more point, originally the title of this book was going to be *Tension Deficit Disorder.* People liked the title very much but it needed explanation. Pastor John Hobratschk lovingly encouraged me to go with "The

Seduction of Extremes" as it was less in need of explanation. I thank him for his wise counsel.

12. It is a painful fact that most of the criticisms against Christianity today are criticisms of kind of a cartoon Homer Simpson version of Christianity. Years ago I was in a debate with a group of witches who blamed me for the Crusades. I told them I was not that old. Also, I told them that much of what was connected with the Crusades was out of step with the gospel so they needed to stop torching useless spiritual scarecrows. Most critics of Christianity don't have the slightest clue of what a gospel-centered Christianity is all about.
13. This contrast of ecumenism with some Christians and not with others is an example that at the same time Christians are called to avoid sectarianism and syncretism. The one is a narrow Christianity with too many boundaries and the other is Christianity with no crucial boundaries. Both create caricatures of a gospel-centered Christianity.
14. While I have deep admiration and gratitude to God for all these theological giants, ultimately Scripture is my interpreter to reality. Each one of them had areas of theological weakness and struggled to apply the gospel to pressing issues of their day. Lewis for example struggled with the gospel facet of the vicarious atonement. Luther once stubbed his theological toe in advising Philip of Hesse secretly to take a second wife. Big oops! Augustine had traces of synergism in his theology. The Bible is a clear book—"a bright lamp shining in a dark place." (2 Peter 1:19) But it is so nuanced that it would take at least three life times of serious study to begin to get the hang of it in terms of doctrine and practice—even with abundant grace. That is why it is so important to be humble in this whole interpretation arena. (Micah 6:8) In the end, any good Bible student must recognize we are pygmies standing on the shoulders of giants.

15. Francis Pieper, *Christian Dogmatics, Vol. 1, (*St. Louis: Concordia Publishing House, 1950), pp. 15-16.
16. Adoph Köberle, *The Quest for Holiness*, (Augsburg Publishing House, 1938). A reprint of this classic can be obtained from Ballast Press, P.O. Box 1193, Evansville Indiana 47706.
17. "Concordia Bible with Notes," (St. Louis: Concordia Publishing House, 1971) p. 343.
18. "Luther's Works," (Volume 18:71 English Edition) LW 18:71.
19. By the way, a subtle but devastating form of salvation by works at work in our culture today is one operated by our school systems. Especially in the sports world of middle school and high school athletics do you see a salvation by works activism being carried out with a fanatical foolishness. You see young people practicing and playing during week nights as late as midnight. You see way too many games, practices that last too long, and parents trying to live vicariously through their children's successes. It is all a virus of salvation by works, legalism, and self-justification. "This is what you must do to put yourself in a right relationship with the coach, teacher, or parent." Again, we see excess and bad theology playing out in the marketplace through lunatic legalism of a very sad order. Added to this, we see kids being treated like slabs of meat at the expense of the ego of coaches. Straining gnats and swallowing camels in the realm of sports, we are creating prematurely crippled young adults—crippled both physically and emotionally.
20. H. Richard Niebuhr, *The Kingdom of God in America*, (New York: Harper and Brothers, 1959), p. 193.
21. Please note that as church bodies abandon a theology of the cross, they become increasingly social clubs and YMCA centers. Consumerism is often the name of the game when it comes to church growth. A theology of glory replaces a theology of Golgotha.
22. Hebrews 11:17.

23. This quote is from F. Scott Fitzgerald's *The Crack-up*, first written in 1936 and published in 1945. The book tells of the sudden descent of Fitzgerald's life at age 39. He goes from apex to nadir.
24. John 18:10-11; Matthew 26:51-54.
25. LW 31:39.
26. Something akin to this paradox is the matter of poison. It is not poison that kills one but the dosage. The law in itself is good. However, if it is taken as dosage for salvation by works, it will serve to act as a lethal poison.
27. Ibid.
28. LW 31:40.
29. Ibid.
30. LW 31:41.
31. Ibid.
32. Heino O. Kadai, editor, *Accents in Luther's Theology*, (St. Louis: Concordia Publishing House, 1967), p. 100.
33. The Biblical support for this is Romans 7:15-24. Here is St. Paul's autobiographical sketch after conversion. It shows the fallout of sin. Any illusions of omnipotence are dashed. Any noxious notions of perfectionism are squashed.
34. Martin H. Scharlemann, *The Paradox in Perspective, Concordia Theological Monthly* Vol. XXXVIII, May 1957, p. 352.
35. LW 43:89.
36. LW 31:344.
37. Lecture notes from a class taught by Dr. Rossow in the summer of 1993, taken while author was doing Doctor of Ministry work at Concordia Seminary in St. Louis, Mo.
38. LW 42:183.
39. LW 21:340.
40. LW 21: pp. 299-300.
41. LW 33: 59.
42. LW 33: 62.

43. LW 33:206.
44. LW 33:168.
45. LW 26:161.
46. LW 26:161.
47. LW 26:162.
48. LW 26:163.
49. Hebrews 4:12-13.
50. LW 8:5-10.
51. LW 8:7-10.
52. LW 8:8-9.
53. LW 8:20.
54. LW 8:207.
55. According to the Lutheran Symbols, the gospel is the center of the Scriptures. For that reason the writers of the Symbols see everything in the Holy Scriptures as related to the gospel in such a way that they can say, "Everything in the Word of God is written down for us, not for the purpose of thereby driving us to despair but in order that 'by steadfastness, by the encouragement of the Scriptures we might have hope' (Romans 15:4)." Tappert edition of *The Book of Concord*, p. 618 (FC SD XI, 12).
56. LW 8:29.
57. Ewald M. Plass, *This is Luther*, (St. Louis: Concordia Publishing House, 1948), p. 325.
58. LW 8:29.
59. Luther catches this paradox when he explains the work of the Holy Spirit in the *Small Catechism*. He wrote to the effect "I believe that I cannot believe." This is the nugget from his larger statement, "I believe that I cannot believe by my own reason or strength, but the Holy Spirit has called me by the gospel."
60. H.C. Leupold, *Expositions of Genesis*, (Grand Rapids: Baker Book House, 1942), p. 43.
61. Leupold, p. 44.

62. Gerhard O. Forde, *Theology Is For Proclamation*, (Minneapolis: Fortress Press, 1990), p. 48.
63. Jay G. Williams, *Ten Words of Freedom*, (Philadelphia: Fortress Press, 1971), p. 101.
64. H.C. Leupold, *Exposition of the Psalms*, (Grand Rapids: Baker Book House, 1969), p. 775, Leupold's translation.
65. Os Guinness, *Prophetic Timeliness*, (Grand Rapids: Baker Books, 2003), p. 49. Guinness quotes C.S. Lewis.
66. Ultimately, the eternity of mankind hinges on Isaiah 53.
67. Throughout the Old Testament, Israel indulged in the outrageous practice of child sacrifice. Even kings like Ahaz passed his son through the fire. (2 Chronicles 28).
68. This group was the Sadducees.
69. In Christendom, we face this same kind of functionalism. Functionalism is where what we do (function) supercedes what God graciously does through the Good News of Messiah Jesus. Functionalism leads into dysfunctionalism. It wears out God's people with endless rules, regulations, cookie-cutter formulas that are simplistic, and layers of bureaucracy. It unwittingly contributes to a lot of professional church worker burnout. This is nothing new under the sun. Utilitarianism often is so impractical.
70. *De Catechizandi's Rudibus* 4.8. This is one of Augustine's earliest works.
71. This is a difficult quote to run down. It is used frequently but rarely attributed. The essence of it can be found in Luther's *Table Talks*. In the 51st paragraph of this collection of Luther's sayings the Reformer says, "Esteem this book as the precious fountain that can never be exhausted. In it thou findest the swaddling-clothes and the manger whither the angels directed the poor, simple shepherds; they seem poor and mean, but dear and precious is the treasure that lies therein." *The Table Talks of Martin Luther*, (New York: Dover Publications 2005) p. 20.

72. Arthur A. Just Jr., *Concordia Commentary on Luke*, (St. Louis: Concordia Publishing House, 1997), Vol. 1, p. 226.
73. *Parousia* is a transliteration of a Greek New Testament word for *coming*. Often it refers to Jesus' glorious second coming. Here we will use it also to refer to how Jesus comes to us today in time and space with his grace.
74. John Bright, *The Kingdom of God*, (Nashville: Abingdon Press, 1953), p. 216.
75. Os Guinness, *Doing Well and Going Good*, (NavPress, Colorado Springs, 2001), p. 29. I am running Guinness' observation meshing it with observations from economist Walt Williams. In the same breath, I must add Guinness' counterbalance observation that U.S. philanthropy is slipping. How can it not when the most powerful motivator for generous giving is waning—the message of the cross?
76. Walter L. Cook, *Meeting the Test*, (Nashville, Abingdon Press, 1960).
77. Note the double paradox. We get happiness by not seeking it and we seek the gift.
78. Voelz, pp. 264-280.
79. Köberle, p. 228.
80. Meekness is not weakness. It is a gentle-strength, hence it is a paradoxical word. It describes the nature of genuine orthodoxy which needs strength and gentleness to be faithful and flexible. Embedded in this concept is the aspect of reasonableness. A reasonable person can see two sides of a given matter. Paradox is ever weighing up the sides and two faces of truth without being two-faced.
81. This is also an important Biblical principle of interpretation. What is descriptive is not necessarily prescriptive. John 3:16 is prescriptive. There is a wonderful whosoever in that powerful promise. Because Jesus walked on water and raised the dead does not mean we have the same authority. Similarly, because the

apostles performed eye-popping miracles and spoke in tongues does not mean we have the same authority. Proclaiming the gospel, administering the sacraments, and showing Christian love is quite prescriptive. Regarding tongues speaking it is certainly possible, but most Christian groups do not follow the apostolic guidelines on this matter: no more than two or three, one at a time, must be an interpretation, don't add or subtract from Scripture, and men only. (1 Corinthians 14:26-40) I have a number of friends that formerly spoke in tongues. In retrospect, they told me that it was something manufactured by man and carnally induced. At the time they spoke in tongues, it was a result of peer pressure. To avoid TDD on this matter, it is best to say we believe and don't believe in tongues today. It all depends in what sense and whether the "tongues" spoken follows the apostolic criteria.

82. Köberle, p. 112.
83. Herman Sasse, *We Confess the Sacraments*, vol. 2 trans. Norman Nagel (St. Louis: Concordia Publishing House, 1985), p. 92.
84. Of ourselves, we have no authority or power to forgive sins. It resides in the power and authority of the risen Savior. With care, we take pains to make this clear in our liturgy as we appropriate this prescriptive gospel gift in our divine worship services. We take a spiritual bath early in the service. It is a royal reminder that the whole life of the Christian is one of continual repentance (Luther's first thesis). Watch the language our Lutheran pastors use: "Upon this your confession, I, by virtue of my office, as a called and ordained servant of the Word, announce the grace of God unto all of you, and in the stead and by the command of my Lord Jesus Christ I forgive you all your sins in the name of the Father and of the Son and of the Holy Spirit." Is it not wonderful that God comforts us with the good news of Jesus in a variety of ways: through the preaching of the gospel, holy baptism, holy communion, love from Christian fellowship, and holy absolution? He knows we need abundant assurances from many angles.

Observe how Jesus bestows this Easter gift of forgiveness. It is so important it is one of the first things he does as risen Lord. He brings peace to fearful disciples. He breathes upon them. He grants them forgiveness. He bestows forgiveness. He commissions them to forgive in his name. He institutes the Office of the Keys by granting them to exercise the keys of forgiveness. This is an awesome authority. It has a prescriptive element. (John 20:21-23). A week later, Thomas will make one of the most complete Christological statements when he confesses Jesus as "My Lord and my God!" (John 20:28). The cults cannot handle this. Yet, it is what it is. The cults will fixate on John 14:29 where Jesus says "the Father is greater than I." To avoid Tension Deficit Disorder, both John 20:28 and John 14:29 must be held in tension. Jesus does this when he says that "I and the Father are one!" The Greek word for *one* means "*one in essence.*" The early church formulated this paradox is a beautiful fashion in The Athanasian Creed, namely, that Jesus was "Equal to the Father as touching His Godhead and inferior to the Father as touching His manhood." (The Lutheran Hymnal, p. 53) This is the way the early church avoided TDD.

85. Martin Luther's *Small Catechism*, the explanation to the person and work of the Holy Spirit, the Third Article.
86. 1 Corinthians 2:9 implies that God is eager to give us even now wonderful gifts far beyond our imagination through his means of grace, baptism, the message of the cross, the Lord's Supper, and holy absolution. ""No eye has seen, nor ear heard, nor the heart of man conceived what God has prepared for those who love him" is not just talking about heaven. Paul's whole letter, carefully read, is a defense of how God wants to stretch our imagination through his means of grace and Jesus' incredible love.
87. Christians live in two kingdoms, the kingdom of Caesar and the kingdom of God. This creates a tension. We are subject to obey two authorities who do not always agree, yet must be obeyed. Romans 13:1-7 must ever be tempered with Acts 5:29.

88. John Bartlett's *Bartlett's Familiar Quotations,* (London: Little, Brown, and Company, 1882, 1980). These words are from Shakespeare's *Macbeth*, V, v, 17.
89. F.F. Bruce, *Commentary on the Book of Acts*, (Grand Rapids: Eerdman's Publishing Co., 1954).
90. Martin Rees, *Our Final Hour,* (New York: Perseus Books Group, 2003), p. 8.
91. *Forbes* magazine, July 17, 1995; pp. 101-102.
92. *Concordia Journal,* July 1995; p. 336.
93. Concordia Bible with Notes (St. Louis: Concordia Publishing House, 1971), p. 61.
94. Gene Edward Veith's *Modern Fascism*, (St. Louis: Concordia Publishing House, 1991).
95. C.S. Lewis' commentary on the value of reading old books in order to understand the new is a good safeguard in our trendy day and age. See introduction to *St. Athanasius on the Incarnation,* (London: A.R. Mowbray, 1953).
96. Scholars have long recognized the book of Revelation is a book loaded with symbols. It is a book by an insider to insiders because of the persecution the early church was enduring. The clearer literal portions of the Bible must interpret the less clear figurative portions unless we follow cult-like procedures in a classic case. Cults always suffer TDD on the person and work of Jesus being especially prone to straining gnats (legalism) as well as minimizing the Lordship of Jesus (swallowing camels). One commentator has put it nicely, "For example, 1,000 (10 x 10 x 10) = completion times completion times completion, indicating ultimate completion; 144,000 (12 x 12 x 10 x 10 x 10)=church (believers) times church (believers) times completion times completion times completion, indicating the number of believers that will go to heaven. Behind this latter symbolism would be: Old Testament church (12 tribes) times New Testament church (12 apostles and their followers) times their complete number times their complete number times their

complete number symbolically equals the total number of Old and New Testament believers who will be saved." Appendixes of Holy Bible (NET) *God's Word To The Nations,* Edition 1992. Regarding the 12 times 12 symbolic numbers of the 144,000, the number that stands for the whole Israel of God, the Israel of Old and the New Israel, the church, (Galatians 6:16) bear in mind that when Jesus (Israel reduced to One) feeds the five thousand, there were 12 baskets of leftovers after this greater-than-the-prophets miracle.

97. Because Jesus is present everywhere as God and man, transcending the time-space continuum, this heightens the awesomeness of his second coming as well as his coming to us today in baptism and the Lord's Supper. In baptism, we are actually incorporated into his body. (1 Corinthians 12:13) In the Lord's Supper, we actually receive his body and blood. (1 Corinthians 10:16) Christ dwells in our body, we are members of his body, and we receive his body in the Lord's Supper and every eye shall see his glorified body on Judgment Day without the aid of cameras, T.V., and video. Then we will be ushered home in glorified bodies to live in the new heaven and new earth for all eternity. (1 Corinthians 15:40-58; Revelation 21:1-4) In the end, Christianity in the best sense is the most materialistic religion. God the Son puts on a body to redeem us body and soul. He grafts us into his body in baptism and gives us his body and blood in the Lord's Supper and dwells within in our body even now. At the end of time, he will take us body and soul to the new heaven and forever new earth in our forever young bodies. No other religion manifests such magnificent concern for the human body like the religion that confesses the body of Christ.

98. Much of fundamentalism today mimics liberal mainstream Christianity and vice versa. How? Each focuses on the peripheral over the core. The temptation for conservative Christians is to focus on certain peripherals to preserve the core. In other words, there is a temptation for them to make things a little tighter than

needs be and go over the cliff on adiaphora (middle things) issues. I will offer an example later on the tricky matter of communion fellowship. Failure to reckon with these trends and temptations is to ignore history as well as the many subtle attacks that the old evil foe launches from all directions.

99. We agree that baptism, the Lord's Supper, and holy absolution have a law component. However, their dominant note is gospel. They are marvelous messianic means by which Jesus bestows His grace upon us here in time.
100. John, in his gospel, records the words of Jesus before Pilate, "My kingship is not of this world." (John 18:36) The word *kingship* is the same word used in John's Revelation 20: 5 when it talks about Jesus' kingship for a thousand years, namely, a kingship not of this world. John's gospel moves us away from a literal 1,000-year earthly rule. Jesus defines the nature of his Kingdom not as power, might, and force, but of faith, weakness, and humility. St. Paul speaks the same way, "For the kingdom of God is not food and drink but righteousness and peace and joy in the Holy Spirit." (Romans 14:17).
101. CTCR Document: *The End Times*, p. 40.
102. By the way, I cannot resist noting the paradox of pluralism. Pluralism—allowing many different religions in a culture—simultaneously, is good and bad. In the context of a fallen world, it is good from the viewpoint of freedom of religion and steering free from state-run churches. It is also simultaneously bad, especially when pluralism becomes synonymous with relativism or becomes a birth mother to fanatical religions that are marked by violence and totalitarian tendencies.
103. William Hendriksen, *More Than Conquerors*, (Grand Rapids: Baker Book House, 1940) p. 190.
104. Herman Sasse, *We Confess the Church*, Vol. 3, trans. Norman Nagel (St. Louis: Concordia Publishing House), p. 111.

105. This is a German and Spanish proverb used in Luther's day. Luther himself put it this way "Where God builds a church, the devil builds a tavern next door." This quote can be found in volume one of *What Luther Says*, a three volume anthology compiled by Ewald Plass, (St. Louis: Concordia Publishing House, 1959), p. 396.
106. John R. Stephenson, *Eschatology*, edited by Robert Preus (Fort Wayne, Indiana: The Luther Academy, 1993), p. 79.
107. *The Book of Concord*, Tappert edition, p. 217.
108. A Sunday school teacher, for example, gets irked by the bad behavior of camel swallowing students. In a moment of weakness the teacher says, "Jesus isn't going to love you any more if you keep acting that way." That is a different gospel, a substitute gospel, a 666 gospel peddled in a moment of weakness by a sinner-saint teacher. It is humbling. Even the best of Christians can lay a theological egg that stinks with elements of a different gospel when it is cracked open. The doctrine of the Antichrist is, once again, a call to see the whole life of a Christian is to be in a state of continuous repentance. After Pentecost, Paul had to pull Peter out of an Antichrist moment. (Galatians 2:11-14).
109. LW 25:380.
110. In this same chapter you have the messianic paradox spoken with irony by the chief priests, scribes, and elders who mocked Jesus while he was on the cross saying, "He saved others; he cannot himself save." (Matthew 27:42) Paradoxically, Jesus drank the full cup of suffering by not drinking from a cup of pain-killer wine mixed with gall. (Matthew 27:33-34) This was the gall of Golgotha.
111. Hal Lindsey, *The Late Great Planet Earth*, pp. 119-135.
112. *John Doe*, personal letter, used with permission, August 1996.
113. The same tension arises throughout the Gospels. Note in Luke 7:14-15 where Jesus is revealed as the healer of all ills. He commands a dead man to stand up. Luke records, "And the dead man

stood up." Here we see the uniqueness of Christianity from one more angle. Only Christianity has a cure for death through the Lord Jesus.

114. The power of the resurrection paradox is foreshadowed in Isaiah 25:8. In light of the New Testament, we see Christ is swallowed up by death in order to swallow up death. (1 Corinthians 15:54).
115. *The Lutheran Agenda* (St. Louis: Concordia Publishing House).
116. The force of the aorist middle imperative in the Greek is one of utmost urgency and joy, "receive my spirit!"
117. LW 4:313.
118. Heinrich Schmid, *The Doctrinal Theology of the Evangelical Lutheran Church*, (Minneapolis: Augsburg Publishing House, 1875), p. 663.
119. Larry Dixon, *The Other Side of the Good News*, (Wheaton, Illinois: Victor Books, 1992).
120. Jurgen Moltmann is a very capable theologian known for his *Theology of Hope* (1964; ET 1967). A German WW II POW for 3 years, Moltmann embraced Jesus Christ as risen Lord while behind barbed wire. He has many salutary insights on the theology of the cross and justification born of serious study and personal trials. Nevertheless, any implication that apart from faith in God's greatest gift to mankind—His crucified Son—one can be saved—misuses the doctrine of justification. It allows universal grace to morph into universalism. This negates the urgent need to believe in so great a salvation, so profound a gift—God's beloved Son crucified for the world (Hebrews 2:1-3). Again, there must be some room for faith and God's scandal of particularity (Deuteronomy 6:4; John 14:6; Acts 4:12).
121. Eliot, by this observation, is also reminding us that universalism destroys the law-gospel paradox by turning the gospel into an *ex opera operato* enterprise where one does not need faith but is saved simply by the outward act of another. Moreover, the deep mystery

and paradox of why some and not others are saved is answered, and the answer, of course, is wrong.

122. Francis Pieper, *Christian Dogmatics* Vol. 3 (St. Louis: Concordia Publishing House, 1953) p. 545.

123. Francis Rossow, *Giving Christian Doctrine a New Translation: Selected Examples from the Novels of C.S. Lewis, Concordia Journal*, July 1995, 287.

124. An end times paradox of interest pertaining to Judgment Day is recorded in Matthew 24:36. Here Jesus declares that in his state of humiliation, he did not know when the end of the world would be. He declares, "But concerning that day and hour no one knows, not even the angels of heaven, nor the Son, but the Father only." Big time paradox! He who knows all things (John 21:17) does not know when the end of the world will take place. Jesus, in a state of humiliation while on earth, must play by the same rules when it comes to walking by faith. He chooses not to use what he knows as God so that he can, in every respect, be tempted as we are. (Hebrews 4:15) The cultists who cannot live with mystery go into severe Tension Deficit Disorder and spin into unbelief declaring Jesus not to be "very God of very God." We, however, rejoice in this and all paradoxes revealed in Scripture as we see them revealing and concealing at the same time.

125. Here again we see the Scripture interprets Scripture, a principle so necessary to avoid TDD.

126. Note that the last book of the Bible is Revelation not Revelations. One of our Seminary professors told us that he would flunk us for the semester if we ever pronounced this last book in the plural. None of us dared to test his resolve. By making such a strong point this wonderful teacher was warning us about revelations beyond Scripture as well as how any preacher on television who speaks of the last book in the plural usually mangles badly this book from St. John. ADD as well as TDD accompanies TV evangelists who speak of Revelation in the plural. The book of Revelation, rightly

understood, is to remind us that we are more than conquerors through Christ who loved us. (Romans 8:37).

127. Köberle, p. 239.
128. ibid.
129. Jim Collins, *Good To Great*, (New York: HarperCollins, 2001).
130. A related paradox comes from Olfer Zur, a therapist who wrote in U.S.A Today on August 3, 2000, these words: "We've become obsessed with speed. We end up with lots of plans that we can't execute, and a full schedule that can't be followed . . . .The paradox of our time-saving tech gadgets is that we have wound up with no free time."
131. Kenneth H. Cooper, M.D. *Can Stress Heal?* (Nashville: Thomas Nelson Publishers, 1997).
132. John Eidsmoe, *Christianity and the Constitution*, (Grand Rapids: Baker Book House Company, 1987). Eidsmoe has read over 100,000 pages of primary source documentation to show the pervasive Christian influence upon our nation's founders. This book as Paul Vitz has written is "a corrective to the almost totally secular portrayal of the Constitution found in so many textbooks today."
133. Eidsmoe, pp. 113-143. I once asked Pulitzer Prize winner and Washington scholar David McCullough what made George Washington tick? After a few seconds of thought he forcefully blurted, "Courage!" Having read many books on Washington, I would agree with McCullough, yet I would like to ask one more vital question. What was the source of Washington's courage? I believe it was the love of Jesus Christ and the hope of heaven that Jesus brings as risen Savior. That is what ultimately made Washington tick. In a speech he made to the Delaware Chiefs on May 12, 1779 Washington said, "You will do well to wish to learn our ways of life, *and above all* (my italics), the religion of Jesus Christ. These will make you a greater and happier people than you are." As a relative to Chief John Shenandoah and part native

American Indian, I take absolutely no umbrage at this statement. While Washington was very discreet in the manner in which he confessed his faith in Jesus, lest he be viewed as a sectarian, his ground of being rested upon the person and work of Jesus Christ. See Eidsmoe page 120 and 130, for the Washington quote and for a beautiful Christ-centered prayer that Washington wrote out by hand and prayed as a young man.

134. Back in 1996, I took a graduate course in Berlin. I spoke to a number of German people who were alive before Hitler came to power. They spoke of how anemic Christianity had been before the rise of Hitler and how sparsely attended church services had become. Read Bonhoeffer's works and you can deduce the same. For over 100 years before the rise of Hitler, a series of "isms" emptied pews and drained people of historic Christian convictions, save for a remnant. Rationalism, nationalism, naturalism, Pietism, theological unionism, Darwinism, and communism all combined to weaken European Christianity. In 1969, I was stunned when my German religion professor at a secular university, a WW II survivor, told me he was an atheist. Technically speaking he was a Lutheran atheist—an ontological oxymoron. Still, that was his human handle. For a chilling picture of the milieu out of which Hitler arose, see Ron Rosenbaum's *Explaining Hitler*, (New York: Random House 1998).
135. Köberle, p. 142.
136. Plass, Vol. 2 *What Luther Says,* p. 561.
137. Jesus wants us to "observe all things whatsoever" he has commanded. This is prescriptive, not descriptive. Within the Great Commission there is great inclusiveness and exclusiveness at the same time. Another paradox, another tension arises.
138. Ralph Bohlmann, Letter to Pastors, July 1988.
139. *Lutheran Forum,* Vol. 28, No. 1, Spring 2004, p. 50.
140. *Lutheran Forum*, Vol. 28, No. 1, Spring 2004, for attribution to this observation by C.S. Lewis. Vicar Louis A Smith has an

excellent article on this subject as he evaluates how the ordination of women has had some unintended consequences in ushering in a different gospel in many quarters of the Evangelical Lutheran Church of America. For more of Lewis' thoughts on this subject see his *God in the Dock,* "Priestesses in the Church?" treatise, 1948. Especially see paragraph 3, 8-9, 11-13, pp. 235-239. Here Lewis is very prophetic and that usually means politically incorrect.

141. ibid.
142. The order of creation (1 Timothy 2:11-3:6) and the order of redemption (Galatians 3:26-28) must be held in tension, lest Tension Deficit Disorder leads to a fountain of different gospels that are no gospels at all. Wherever these orders are not held in tension, legalism and lawlessness slither into the church bringing disorder and oppression of numerous kinds.
143. Os Guinness *Fit Bodies Fat Minds—Why Evangelicals Don't Think and What to Do About It* (Grand Rapids: Baker Book House Co. 1994), p. 12.
144. *Blaise Pascal and the Relevance of His Christian Writings*, edited by James M. Houston, (Colorado Springs: Victor, 2006), p. 221.
146. So curious readers will not be frustrated as to the top five songs from U.S. films they are: 1) *"Over the Rainbow"* 1939; *"As Time Goes By"* from "*Casablanca,"* 1942; *"Singing in the Rain"* from the movie with the same name, 1952; "*Moon River"* from "*Breakfast at Tiffany's,"* 1961; and *"White Christmas"* from "*Holiday Inn,"* 1942. I would offer the opinion that those songs of yesteryear came from an era that, like ours, had immense challenges but through the wholesome influence of the gospel did not suffer nearly the TDD that our age is suffering.
147. Köberle, pp. 262-263.
148. This quote comes from *The Paradoxes of Group Life*, (San Francisco: Jossey-Bass Publishers, 1987, 1997) p. 3. Two authors wrote this book: David N. Berg and Kenwyn K. Smith. They argue that paradox is a tool to be used as a guide for grasping reality. They use

paradox as a means and way of conceptualizing reality, especially as it relates to group dynamics.

Pleasant
Word

Printed in the United States
150515LV00007B/25/A

9 781414 106441